Look Homeward, Angel

A COMEDY-DRAMA IN THREE ACTS

By Ketti Frings

Based on the Novel
by Thomas Wolfe

Winner, Pulitzer Prize, 1958;
New York Critics' Award, 1958

SAMUEL FRENCH, INC.

45 WEST 25TH STREET   NEW YORK 10010
7623 SUNSET BOULEVARD   HOLLYWOOD 90046
LONDON   *TORONTO*

LOOK HOMEWARD, ANGEL

Presented by Kermit Bloomgarden and Theatre 200, Inc., at the Ethel Barrymore Theatre, New York City, November 28th, 1957, with the following cast:

BEN GANT	_Arthur Hill_
MRS. MARIE "FATTY" PERT	_Florence Sundstrom_
HELEN GANT BARTON	_Rosemary Murphy_
HUGH BARTON	_Leonard Stone_
ELIZA GANT	_Jo Van Fleet_
WILL PENTLAND	_Tom Flatley Reynolds_
EUGENE GANT	_Anthony Perkins_
JAKE CLATT	_Joseph Bernard_
MRS. CLATT	_Mary Farrell_
FLORRY MANGLE	_Elizabeth Lawrence_
MRS. SNOWDEN	_Julia Johnston_
MR. FARREL	_Dwight Marfield_
MISS BROWN	_Susan Torrey_
LAURA JAMES	_Frances Hyland_
W. O. GANT	_Hugh Griffith_
DR. MAGUIRE	_Victor Kilian_
TARKINTON	_Jack Sheehan_
MADAME ELIZABETH	_Bibi Osterwald_
LUKE GANT	_Arthur Storch_

Directed by GEORGE ROY HILL

Settings and Lighting Designed by JO MIELZINER

Costumes by MOTLEY

Production Stage Manager, KERMIT KEGLEY

3

SYNOPSIS OF SCENES

The town of Altamont, in the State of North Carolina, in the fall of the year nineteen hundred and sixteen.

ACT ONE

SCENE 1:
The Dixieland Boarding House; a fall afternoon.

SCENE 2:
The same; that evening.

ACT TWO

SCENE 1:
Gant's marble yard and shop; one week later.

SCENE 2:
The Dixieland Boarding House; the next night.

ACT THREE

The Dixieland Boarding House; two weeks later.

Look Homeward, Angel

ACT ONE

SCENE 1

SCENE: *The Dixieland Boarding House; a fall afternoon.*
The house is a flimsily constructed frame house of
fifteen draughty, various-sized rooms. It has a ram-
bling, unplanned gabular appearance, and is painted
a dirty yellow. Most of its furniture is badly worn and
out of style. The beds are chipped enamel-covered
iron. There are accordion hat trees, cracked mir-
rors, an occasional plant. On the typically Southern
veranda which embraces the front and one side of
the house, there are chairs, rockers, and a wood box.
There is a sign above the door, electrically lighted
at night: DIXIELAND—ROOMS AND BOARD. *In the Cen-*
ter of the house, slightly raised, is a turntable on
which all the bedroom scenes are played. At the back
of the house a walk approaches the rear of the
veranda. There is a side door and near it a circular
yard seat. Also Down front of the bedroom is a table
and a chair. The street itself has a feeling of great
trees hanging over it. Occasionally during the play,
the stillness is broken by the rustle of autumn leaves,
and the poignant wail of a train whistle. The Curtain
rises in darkness. After a moment we hear EUGENE'S
voice coming from his room. Seated, he is glimpsed,
writing, surrounded by books.

EUGENE. "Ben" by Eugene Gant. . . . My brother
Ben's face is like a piece of slightly yellow ivory. (*Lights*
come up on the veranda where BEN GANT, *30, delicate*
and sensitive, the most refined of the Gants, and forever
a stranger among them, is seated on the front steps read-

ing a newspaper. He is sometimes scowling and surly, but he is the hero protector of those he loves, with quiet authority and a passion for home which is fundamental. At times he speaks to the side over his shoulder, in a peculiar mannerism of speech, as though he were address-ing a familiar unseen presence.)

His high, white forehead is knotted fiercely by an old
    man's scowl.
His mouth is like a knife.
His smile the flicker of light across the blade.
His face is like a blade, and a knife, and a flicker of light.
And when he fastens his hard white fingers
And his scowling eyes upon a thing he wants to fix,
He sniffs with sharp and private concentration.
(*Lights now reveal* MARIE "FATTY" PERT, *43, seated near* BEN *in her rocker. She is a generous, somewhat boozy woman, knitting a pair of men's socks and ten-derly regarding* BEN.)
Thus women looking, feel a well of tenderness
For his pointed, bumpy, always scowling face. . . .
(EUGENE *continues writing.*)

BEN. Somebody's got to drive the Huns from the skies. Poor old England can't be expected to do it alone.

MRS. PERT. It's their mess, isn't it?

BEN. It says here there's an American flying corps forming in Canada.

MRS. PERT. Ben Gant, what are you thinking of?

BEN. All my life in this one little burg, Fatty! Besides getting away, I'd be doing my bit.

MRS. PERT. Would they take you so old?

BEN. This article says eighteen to thirty-two.

MRS. PERT. Aren't the physical standards pretty high?

BEN. Listen to her! I'm in good condition!

MRS. PERT. You're twenty pounds underweight! I never saw anyone like you for not eating.

BEN. Maguire gave me a thorough checkup this spring!

MRS. PERT. How would your family feel if you went?

BEN. What family? The batty boarders? (*Takes her hand.*) Apologies, Fatty. I never associate you with them. Except for Gene, nobody'd know I was gone. (*Looks up, dreamily.*) To fly up there in the wonderful world of the sky. Up with the angels.

(HELEN GANT BARTON *and her husband* HUGH *enter from the house.* HELEN *is gaunt, raw-boned, in her middle twenties, often nervous, intense, irritable and abusive, though basically generous, the hysteria of excitement constantly lurking in her. It is a spiritual and physical necessity for her to exhaust herself in service to others, though her grievances, especially in her service to her mother, are many.* HUGH *is a cash register salesman, simple, sweet, extremely warmhearted. He carries a newspaper, a tray with a coffee pot and cups and saucers, which* HELEN *helps him set on a table. They have been arguing.*)

HUGH. We should never have agreed to live here for one day—that's the answer. You work yourself to the bone—-for what?

HELEN. (*Busy putting cups in saucers.*) Mrs. Pert, the other boarders have almost finished dinner!

MRS. PERT. What's the dessert, Helen?

HELEN. Charlotte Russe.

HUGH. They're like children with a tapeworm. (*Crosses and sits woodbox Down Right.*)

BEN. Fatty, I told you you'd better get in there!

MRS. PERT. I was trying to do without, but I'm afraid that calls me. (*Rises.*) See you later, Ben. (*She leaves her knitting on the chair, exits inside.*)

HELEN. Ben, where is Mama?

BEN. How should I know?

HELEN. I've had to serve the entire dinner alone!

HUGH. Look at me, holes in my socks, a trouser button missing—and before I married you I had the reputation of being "dapper."

HELEN. I bet she's off somewhere with Uncle Will, and

I'm left in the kitchen to slave for a crowd of old cheap boarders! That's her tactic!

HUGH. "Dapper Hugh Barton"—it said so in the newspaper when we were married.

HELEN. (*Crosses to* BEN, *who pays no attention.*) You know that, don't you, *don't you?* And do I ever hear her say a word of thanks? Do I get—do I get as much as a go-to-hell for it? No. "Why, pshaw, child," she'll say, "I work more than anybody!" And most times, damn her, she does.

BOARDERS. (*Offstage, calling, ringing the service bell.*) Helen. Helen!

HELEN. You come in, Hugh, and help me! (*Exits into the house.*)

BEN. How are the cash registers selling, Hugh?

HUGH. Putting the cigar box out of business. I got a good order in Raleigh last week. I've already put away nine hundred dollars toward our own little house.

BEN. (*Rises.*) You ought to have one, Hugh. You and Helen. (*Crossing toward wicker unit Down Left where he has left his coat.*)

HUGH. (*Looking at part of newspaper.*) I guess they don't have to advertise the good jobs, do they? The really big jobs—they wouldn't be here in the newspaper, would they?

BEN. Why?

HUGH. If there was something good here in town—not cn the road so much—maybe then I could talk Helen into moving away. Ben— (*Rises.*) you hear things around the paper—

HELEN. (*Off.*) Hugh! Hugh!

BEN. I'll keep my ears open, Hugh.

HUGH. Well, I guess I don't want to make Helen any madder at me. Thanks, Ben. (*Exits inside.*)

(*An AUTOMOBILE is heard off, driving up, stopping. BEN moves down to the yard seat, reads his newspaper. The CAR DOOR slams.*)

ELIZA. (*Off.*) I'll vow I never saw such a man. What little we have got, I've had to fight for tooth and nail, tooth and nail! (ELIZA GANT *enters with* WILL PENTLAND, *her brother.* ELIZA, *57, is of Scotch descent, with all the acquisitiveness and fancied premonitions of the Scotch. She is mercurial, with dauntless energy, greed and love. She has an odd way of talking, pursing her lips, and she characteristically uses her right hand in a point-making gesture, fist enclosed, forefinger extended. These mannerisms are often imitated by those who hate and love her.* ELIZA *is carrying some fall leaves, a real estate circular and two small potted plants.* WILL *is paunchy, successful, secure, a real estate broker. He carries a small tray with several flower pots, geranium cuttings, and a can of peat moss therein, which he places on woodbox. They do not notice* BEN.) Like the fellow says, there's no fool like an old fool! Of course Mr. Gant's been a fool all his life. Pshaw! If I hadn't kept after him all these years we wouldn't have a stick to call our own.

WILL. You had to have an "artistic" husband. (*Places flower pots on table above* PERT'S *rocker.*)

ELIZA. (*Crosses to Left of* WILL.) Artistic. I have my opinion about that. Why, Will, the money that man squanders every year on liquor alone would buy all kinds of good downtown property, to say nothing of paying off this place. We could be well-to-do people now if we'd started at the very beginning.

WILL. (*He fixes a cutting into one of the pots and places it on the porch rail Right.*) You've given him every opportunity.

ELIZA. He's always hated the idea of owning anything—couldn't bear it, he told me once—'cause of some bad trade he made when he was a young man up in Pennsylvania. If I'd been in the picture then, you can bet your bottom dollar there'd been no loss.

WILL. (*Chuckling.*) Or the loss'd been on the other side.

ELIZA. (*Moving him front of her to the steps.*) That's

a *good* one! You know us Pentlands! Well, I'm going to
get after Mr. Gant right today about that bank offer.

WILL. (*In yard Right of Right porch pillar.*) Let me
know when you've warmed him up enough for me to talk
to him.

ELIZA. (*On porch step.*) It'll take a good deal of warm-
ing up, I can tell you. He's so blamed stubborn about
that precious old marble yard, but I'll do it!

WILL. Give me a jingle when you want to look at that
farm property. (*Exiting.*) I'll drive you out there.

ELIZA. Thanks, Will! I appreciate it. (*Places leaves,
brochure and purse on Left porch pillar. Sees* BEN.) Ben!
What are you doing home at this hour?

BEN. I'm working afternoons this week.

ELIZA. Oh. (*Somewhat worriedly. Crossing onto porch
for two small flower pots.*) Will you get dinner downtown?

BEN. I usually do.

ELIZA. (*Crossing into yard to Right of Center table.*)
You always sound so short with me, Ben. Why is that?
You don't even look at me. You know I can't stand not
being looked at by the person I'm talking to. Don't you
feel well?

BEN. I feel good.

(*A TRAIN WHISTLE is heard in the distance.*)

ELIZA. Oh, pshaw, there's the midday train now! Has
Eugene gone to the station?

BEN. How should I know?

ELIZA. (*Crossing Left. Calling up to* EUGENE's *room.*)
Eugene, are you up in your room? Eugene? (EUGENE,
*hearing his mother's voice, rises from his chair, turns
toward the window, but he doesn't answer, and* ELIZA
does not see him. EUGENE *is 17, the youngest of the
Gants, tall, awkward, with a craving for knowledge and
love. During the following he leaves his room. Crossing
toward porch Right.*) Eugene! I'll vow, that boy! Just
when I need him— (*Notices* MRS. PERT's *knitting.*) Ben.

I hope you haven't been lying around here wasting time with that Mrs. Pert again?

BEN. Listen to her! It's the nicest time I spend.

ELIZA. (*Crossing to Right of him.*) I tell you what: it doesn't look right, Ben. What must the other boarders think? A woman her age—a drinking woman—married. Can't you find someone young and pretty and free to be with? I don't understand it. You're the best looking boy I've got.

BEN. (*More pleasantly.*) If it'll make you feel better, Mama, I'll look around.

ELIZA. (*Relieved by the change in his mood, smiles. She also notices the sprawled newspaper. Crossing to Right of Center table.*) That's Mr. Clatt's newspaper. You know he's finicky about reading it first. Fold it up before you go. (*During the above,* EUGENE *is seen coming down the stairs from his room. Now limping slightly, he starts to sneak out the side door, but* ELIZA *spots him.*) Eugene, where are you sneaking to? Come out here.

EUGENE. (*Comes out to Left of Center table.*) Yes, Mama?

ELIZA. The train's just coming in. Now you hurry over to that depot.

EUGENE. Today? I did it yesterday.

ELIZA. Every day until every room is filled. The advertising cards are on the hall table. Go get them. (EUGENE, *disgruntled, goes into the entry hall to get the cards from a small stand.* ELIZA *strips some dead leaves off a plant.*) I declare, seventeen is an impossible age. I don't know why he complains. He hasn't anything else to do. Spending his time up there scribbling, dreaming.

BEN. The other boarding houses send their porters to the trains.

ELIZA. Never you mind, Ben Gant, you used to do it. It's little enough I've ever asked of you boys. (*To* EUGENE *as he comes from the hall.*) Have you got the cards? (*Crossing onto porch to flower tray.*)

EUGENE. (*Crossing Left.*) In my pocket.

ELIZA. (*Holding out her hand.*) Let me see them. Let me see them!

EUGENE. (*In yard front of Left pillar. Takes cards from pocket, reads.*) "Stay at Dixieland, Altamount's Homiest Boarding House."—It should be homeliest.

ELIZA. Eugene!

EUGENE. I hate drumming up trade! It's deceptive and it's begging.

ELIZA. Oh my—my! Dreamer Eugene Gant, what do you think the world is all about? We are all—all of us —selling something. Now you get over to the depot right this minute. And for heaven's sake, boy, spruce up, shoulders back! Look like you *are* somebody! (EUGENE *starts off.*) And smile! Look pleasant! (EUGENE *grins, maniacally.*)

BEN. (*Suddenly, as he watches* EUGENE *limping.*) Gene! What are you walking like that for?

EUGENE. Like what?

BEN. (*Rises.*) What are you limping for? My God, those are my shoes you've got on! I threw them out yesterday!

ELIZA. (*Busy at flower tray.*) They're practically brand new.

BEN. They're too small for *me*, they must be killing him.

EUGENE. Ben, please!

ELIZA. (*Takes flower tray to Up Right table.*) Maybe you can afford to throw out brand-new shoes.

BEN. Mama, for God's sake, you ask him to walk straight, how can he? His toes must be like pretzels!

EUGENE. They're all right. I'll get used to them.

BEN. (*Throwing down his paper.*) My God, it's a damned disgrace, sending him out on the streets like a hired man. Gene should be *on* that train, going to college!

ELIZA. (*Crossing to Right of Center table with can of peat moss.*) That's enough—that's just enough of that! You haven't a family to provide for like I have, Ben Gant. Now I don't want to hear another word about it!

Gene will go to college when we can afford it. This year he can help his Papa at the shop.

BEN. I thought you were going to "warm up" Papa, so he'll sell the shop.

ELIZA. Ben Gant, that wasn't intended for your ears. I'd appreciate it if you wouldn't mention it to Mr. Gant until I have. Hurry off now, son, get us a customer!

EUGENE. (*Crossing to Left of Center table.*) Why should Papa sell his shop?

ELIZA. (*Packing moss in flower pots.*) Now, you're too young to worry about my business. You tend to yours.

EUGENE. What business do I have to attend to, Mama?

ELIZA. Well, get busy, get busy! Help your Papa at the shop.

EUGENE. I don't want to be a stonecutter.

ELIZA. Well, go back to delivering newspapers. Work for Uncle Will in his real estate office. But keep the ball rolling, child. Now hurry on or you'll be late! (EUGENE *exits.*)

HELEN. (*Entering from hall Right.*) Mama, dinner's practically over! I'm no slave!

ELIZA. I'll be right in, Helen. (HELEN *exits, slamming door.* ELIZA *sighs. For a moment, left alone with* BEN, *she becomes herself, a deeply troubled woman.*) What's the matter with him, Ben? What's wrong with that boy? (*Crosses to pillar for purse, leaves and brochure.*) What's the matter with all of you? I certainly don't know. I tell you what, sometimes I get frightened. Seems as if every one of you's at the end of something, dissatisfied, and wants something else. But it just can't be. A house divided against itself cannot stand. I'll vow, I don't know what we're all coming to. (*Approaches side door Left, pauses.*) If you like, this once, as long as you're home, why don't you eat here? I'm sure there's plenty left over.

BEN. No, thank you, Mama. (*He starts off.*)

ELIZA. A good hot meal!

BEN. (*Tosses paper on Center table.*) I've got to get over there.

ELIZA. Ben, are you sure you feel all right?

BEN. I feel fine.

ELIZA. Well, have a nice day at the paper, son.

(BEN *exits.* ELIZA *looks after him, then hearing the voices of the* BOARDERS, *exits into the house by the side door. The* BOARDERS, *ushered by* HELEN, *enter through the front door. They are:* JAKE CLATT, *30, an insensitive boor.* MRS. CLATT, *60,* JAKE'S *mother, with a coarse smile and dyed hair. She is deaf and carries a cane.* FLORRY MANGLE, *29, wistful, humorless, interested in* JAKE. MRS. SNOWDEN, *50, quiet, unobtrusive, lonely. Takes her coffee, sits Up Right.* MISS BROWN, *36, prim on the surface, but with the marks of the amateur prostitute.* MR. FARREL, *60, a retired dancing master, new to Dixieland.*)

MRS. CLATT. I ate too much again.

HELEN. (*Loudly to* MRS. CLATT, *as she crosses to table with fresh pot of coffee.*) Help yourself to coffee, please, Mrs. Clatt. I'm short-handed today.

MRS. CLATT. (*Brandishing her cane at* MR. FARREL, *who is about to sit chair Down Right.*) Not there, that's my chair! That one's free, since the school teacher left.

MISS BROWN. (*At front of porch door.*) You're a teacher too, aren't you, Mr. Farrel?

MR. FARREL. Of the dance. Retired.

MISS BROWN. I hope you'll stay with us for a while. Where are you from?

MR. FARREL. Tampa.

MISS BROWN. Do you know the Castle Walk, Mr. Farrel? I'd love to learn it! (*They stroll down to the yard seat Left.*)

MRS. CLATT. I don't know what Mrs. Gant makes this coffee of. (*Crosses, sits Down Right.*) There isn't a bean invented tastes like this.

JAKE. (*On porch Up Right Center.*) Couldn't you make it for us sometime, Helen?

HELEN. My mother always makes the coffee here.

(HUGH *and* MRS. PERT *enter. The* OTHERS *seat themselves.*)

MRS. PERT. That was scrumptious dessert, but oh dear! (*Sits in her rocker.*)

JAKE. (*Down Right Center on porch.*) Yes, it was good, if only the servings were bigger.

MRS. CLATT. I'm told the best boarding house food in town is down the street at Mrs. Haskell's.

JAKE. That's right, Mother. That's what I heard.

HUGH. (*Crossing to yard to Left of* MRS. PERT.) Then move in to Mrs. Haskell's!

HELEN. (*With a shove.*) Hugh! (*She exits.*)

MISS MANGLE. (*Seated Right of door.*) I spent one season there, but I prefer it here. It's more informal and entertaining.

JAKE. (*Seated woodbox.*) Not lately. It's been over a month since Mrs. Gant had to have Mr. Molasses Edward, and his two Dixie Ramblers evicted for not paying their rent. She certainly loves to see the police swarm around!

(LAURA JAMES, *23, carrying a suitcase, and a Dixieland advertising card, enters. She is attractive, but not beautiful. She advances to the steps.*)

MISS MANGLE. Don't you?

JAKE. I like excitement—why shouldn't I?

MISS MANGLE. Other people's excitement. Don't you ever want excitement of your own? I do.

(MRS. CLATT *sees* LAURA; *nudges her son into attention.* HUGH *turns to her.*)

LAURA. Good afternoon!

HUGH. Good afternoon!

LAURA. Is the proprietor here?

HUGH. I'll call her. (*Calls inside.*) Mrs. Gant! Customer! (*To* LAURA.) Please come right up.

JAKE. (*Leaping to* LAURA.) Here, let me take that suitcase. It must be heavy for you.

LAURA. Thank you.

(JAKE *takes* LAURA'S *suitcase. Puts it on porch Right of Right pillar. The other* BOARDERS *look her over, whisper.* ELIZA, *wearing an apron, places the leaves in a vase on the hall table, enters. At first raking glance she doubts that* LAURA, *so young and different, is a true prospect.*)

ELIZA. Yes?

LAURA. Are you the proprietor?

ELIZA. Mrs. Eliza Gant—that's right.

LAURA. (*Crossing to Left of* ELIZA *on porch.*) I found this card on the sidewalk.

ELIZA. (*Takes card.*) On the sidewalk! And you're looking for a room?

LAURA. If you have one for me.

ELIZA. (*Taking her to chair Left of Center table which* HUGH *has pulled out for her.*) Of course I have, dear—a nice quiet room. You just sit down here and have yourself a cup of my *good* coffee, while I go and open it up, so I can show it to you. Hugh, you take care of the young lady. This is Mr. Barton, my son-in-law.

LAURA. How do you do, Mr. Barton? I'm Laura James.

ELIZA. (*Turns at steps.*) Laura—why that's a *good* Scotch name. Are you Scotch?

LAURA. On one side.

ELIZA. (*Crosses back to her.*) Pshaw! I could have told you were Scotch the minute I laid eyes on you. I'm Scotch too. Well, isn't that nice? (*Makes introductions.* HUGH *crosses porch for coffee.*) Miss James, Mr. Clatt— (*Each acknowledges the introduction according to his personality.*) His mother, Mrs. Clatt, Mrs. Snowden, Miss Mangle, Mr. Farrel— (*Disapprovingly notices* MISS BROWN *flirting with* MR. FARREL.) Miss Brown—Miss Brown! and Mrs. Pert. Where do you come from, dear?

LAURA. I live in Richmond.

(MISS BROWN *and* MR. FARREL *exit Down Right practicing the Castle Walk, eventually reappear at the rear of the veranda Up Right.*)

ELIZA. Richmond! Now that's a pleasant city—but hot! Not like it is here, cool and refreshing in these hills. You haven't come to Altamont for a cure, have you, dear?

LAURA. I'm healthy, if that's what you mean. But I've been working hard and I need a rest.

ELIZA. (*As* HUGH *approaches with coffee.*) Here's your coffee.

LAURA. (*Takes coffee.*) Thank you, Mr. Barton. What are your rates, Mrs. Gant?

EUGENE. (*Off.*) Mama! Mama! (*Runs up the back walk, around the veranda.*)

ELIZA. Suppose I show you the room first.

EUGENE. Mama!

ELIZA. (*Crossing above* LAURA *to Right of her.*) I declare that child either crawls like a snail or speeds like a fire engine

EUGENE. (*Pulls* ELIZA *off Left away from the others.*) Can I speak to you, Mama?

ELIZA. I don't see you limping *now,* when you're not trying to get sympathy. Don't think I don't know your little tricks to—

EUGENE. (*Urgently.*) Mama, Papa's been at Laughran's again. Doctor Maguire is trying to steer him home now.

ELIZA. (*Momentarily stabbed.*) The doctor? Is he sick or is he drunk?

EUGENE. He's rip roaring! He's awful. He kicked Uncle Will again!

(HUGH *and* JAKE *have seated* LAURA *Left of Center table*—LAURA *removes her hat. Offstage are the sounds of a SMALL RIOT approaching. The occasional bull yell of* GANT, CHILDREN *chanting "Old Man Gant came home drunk," a dog barking, etc.*)

ELIZA. (*Weakly.*) I don't think I can stand it again. A *new* young lady, too. (EUGENE *turns to see* LAURA, *who, with the other* BOARDERS, *have heard the approaching* GANT.) Oh Eugene, why do they keep bringing him home? Take him to a state institution, throw him in the gutter, I don't care. I don't know what to do any more. What'll I do, child?

EUGENE. At least it's been a month this time.

GANT. (*Off.*) Mountain Grills! Stay away from me!

JAKE CLATT. My God, Mr. Gant's on the loose again! (*Crosses onto porch.*)

MISS MANGLE. Oh dear, oh dear—

MRS. CLATT. What? What is it?

JAKE CLATT. (*Shouting.*) The old boy's on the loose again!

EUGENE. (*Crossing Up to the* BOARDERS.) Would you go inside, all of you, please?

MRS. CLATT. I haven't finished my coffee.

EUGENE. You can wait in the parlor. Please, just until we get him upstairs!

JAKE CLATT. (*Crosses porch Up Right.*) And miss the show?

MISS BROWN. Come along, Mr. Farrel. Let's clear the deck for the old geezer.

MR. FARREL. Perhaps there is some way I can help?

MISS BROWN. I wouldn't recommend it, Mr. Farrel.

JAKE CLATT. Look at him, he's really got a snootful this time!

(EUGENE *urges several of the* BOARDERS *inside, where they cram in the hallway.* JAKE *and* MRS. CLATT *remain on the porch.* LAURA, *not knowing where to go, remains with* HUGH *outside.*)

GANT. (*From up the walk in the back, bellowing like a wounded bull. Off.*) Mountain Grills! Mountain Grills! Fiends, not friends! Don't push me! *Get away from me!*

DR. MAGUIRE. (*Off.*) All right then, Gant, if you can walk, walk! (ELIZA *stands Downstage, stiff and straight.*

W. O. GANT, *60, clatters up the back veranda steps, his
arms flailing. At heart he is a far wanderer and a minstrel
but he has degraded his life with libertinism and drink.
In him still, though, there is a monstrous fumbling for
life. He is accompanied by* DR. MAGUIRE, *unkempt but
kind, and by* TARKINTON, *disreputably dressed, a crony,
also drunk but navigating, and by* WILL PENTLAND.)
Here we are, Gant; let's go in the back way.

(WILL *precedes* GANT *and crosses to yard Down Right.*
     GANT *pushes the* DOCTOR *aside, plunges headlong
     along the veranda, scattering rockers, flower pots,
     etc.*)

GANT. Where are you? Where are you? The lowest of
the low—boarding house swine! Merciful God, what a
travesty! That it should come to this! (*Stumbles, almost
falls, bursts into maniacal laughter.*)

EUGENE. Papa, come on—Papa, please! (EUGENE *tries
to take* GANT *by the arm;* GANT *flings him aside.*)

GANT. (*With a sweeping gesture.*)
              "Waken lords and ladies gay
              On the mountain dawns the day—"
(*Stumbles,* GENE *catches him.* MRS. CLATT *screams and
dashes into the hall.*) Don't let me disturb your little
tate-a-tete. Go right ahead, help yourself. (*Tosses* GENE
toward PERT'S *rocker.*) Another helping of mashed pota-
toes, Mrs. Clatt? Put another tire around your middle—
(EUGENE *tries to catch* GANT'S *flailing arms.*)

ELIZA. (*Crossing to Left of Left pillar.*) Mr. Gant, I'd
be ashamed, I'd be ashamed.

GANT. Who speaks?

ELIZA. I thought you were sick.

GANT. I am not sick, Madame; I am in a wild, blind
fury. (*Raises a chair aloft, threatening* ELIZA. EUGENE
and the DOCTOR *grab it away from him.* LAURA, *urged
by* HUGH, *retreats to Down Left unit.*)

ELIZA. Dr. Maguire, get him in the house.

DR. MAGUIRE. (*Right of* GANT.) Come on, Gant, let me help you.

GANT. Just one moment! You don't think I know my own home when I see it? This is not where I live. I reside at *92 Woodson Street.*

DR. MAGUIRE. That was some years ago. This is your home now, Gant.

GANT. This barn? This damnable, this awful, this murderous and bloody barn—home! Holy hell, what a travesty on nature! A-h-h-h! (*He maniacally lunges to the yard after* ELIZA. GENE *halts him.*)

WILL. Why don't we carry him in?

DR. MAGUIRE. You keep out of this, Pentland. You're the one who enrages him.

GANT. (*Tossing* GENE *onto steps.*) Pentland—now that's a name for you! (*Pivots, searching for him.*) Where are you, Will Pentland? (*Sees him, staggers toward him.*) You're a Mountain Grill! Your father was a Mountain Grill and a horse thief, and he was hanged in the public square.

(*While* HUGH *holds* GANT, EUGENE *brings a cup of coffee.*)

EUGENE. (*Left of* GANT.) Papa, wouldn't you like some coffee? There's some right here.

GANT. Hah! Some of Mrs. Gant's *good* coffee? (*He kicks at the coffee cup.* EUGENE *backs away.*) Ahh! I'll take some of that *good* bourbon, if you have it, son.

DR. MAGUIRE. (*Crosses, puts bag on* PERT *rocker.*) Get him a drink! Maybe he'll pass out.

GANT. Drink!

ELIZA. (*Stopping* GENE *at door.*) Gene! Dr. Maguire, you know there isn't a drop of alcohol in this house!

LAURA. I have some. (LAURA *quickly opens her handbag, takes from it a small vial, crosses to the* DOCTOR.) I always carry it in case of a train accident.

GANT. (*Lunges toward her.*) Well, what are we waiting for, let's have it!

DR. MAGUIRE. (*Taking the vial.*) Good God, this won't fill one of his teeth.

GANT. (*Roars.*) Well, let's have it! (LAURA *backs away in fear.*)

DR. MAGUIRE. You can have it, Gant—but you'll have to come up onto the veranda to drink it—

GANT. Mountain Grills! Vipers! Lowest of the low! I'll stand here until you take me home. (HELEN *enters from Up Right.*) Isn't anybody going to take me home?

HELEN. (*Crossing to Right of* GANT.) Papa! Why have you been drinking again when you know what it does to you?

GANT. (*Weakens, leans against her.*) Helen—I have a pain right here.

HELEN. Of course you do. Come with me now. I'll put you to bed, and bring you some soup. (HELEN *takes the huge man's arm, leads him toward the veranda.* HELEN's *success with* GANT *etches itself deeply into* ELIZA's *face.*)

GANT. (*Weakly.*) Got to sit down— (*Sits on edge of porch, Left of Left pillar, pats space beside him.*) Sit down, Helen, you and me. (*She sits step Right of* GANT. GENE *sits table Left of* GANT.) Sit and talk. Would you like to hear some Keats—beautiful Keats?

ELIZA. (*Crossing Up to veranda, angrily.*) He's got his audience now. That's all he wants.

EUGENE. Mama, he's sick!

ELIZA. (*On porch step.*) Mr. Gant, if you feel so bad, why don't you act nice and go inside? The whole neighborhood's watching you.

GANT. (*Wildly sings.*)

"Old man Gant came home drunk—"

(TARKINTON *joins him.*)

"Old man Gant came home drunk—"

TARKINTON. (*Singing, waving his arms. Seated chair which* GENE *had taken from* GANT *and placed Left of woodbox.*)

"Old man Gant came home—"

(*His joy fades as he sees* ELIZA *glaring at him.*)

ELIZA. Were you drinking with him too, Mr. Tarkinton?

TARKINTON. Sev-ereral of us were, Mrs. Gant, I regret to say.

ELIZA. (*Pulling* TARKINTON *to his feet.*) I'll have Tim Laughran thrown in jail for this.

TARKINTON. He started out so peaceable like—

ELIZA. (*Pushing him toward Rear exit of veranda.*) I've warned him for the last time.

TARKINTON. Just on beer!

ELIZA. *Get off my premises!*

(TARKINTON *exits.* GANT *groans.* DOCTOR *to yard Right of* HELEN.)

HELEN. Dr. Maguire's here to give you something for your pain, Papa.

GANT. Doctors! Thieves and bloodsuckers! (DOCTOR *crosses to bag.*) "The paths of glory lead but to the grave."—Gray's Elegy. Only four cents a letter on any tombstone you choose, by the master carver— Any orders? (*He groans with pain.*) It's the devil's own pitchfork. Don't let them put me under the knife—promise me, daughter. Promise me! (HELEN *nods. With a giant effort,* GANT *pulls himself up.*) "Over the stones, rattle his bones! He's only a beggar that nobody owns."

DR. MAGUIRE. Good God, he's on his feet again.

EUGENE. Hugh, let's get him in the house.

GANT. (*Throwing off* HUGH *and* EUGENE.) I see it! I see it! Do you see the Dark Man's shadow? There! There he stands—the Grim Reaper—as I always knew he would. So you've come at last to take the old man home? Jesus, have mercy on my soul! (GANT *falls to the ground. There is an agonized silence.* EUGENE, THE DOCTOR, *and* HUGH *rush to him.*)

ELIZA. (*Anxiously, above Right pillar.*) Dr. Maguire.

DR. MAGUIRE. (*Feels* GANT'S *heart.*) He's just passed out, Mrs. Gant.

DR. MAGUIRE. Men, let's carry him up!

(HUGH, WILL, MAGUIRE *and* EUGENE *lift the heavy body, quickly carry* GANT *inside.* HELEN *follows.* ELIZA, *saddened and miserable, starts to gather the coffee cups.* LAURA *picks up her suitcase and starts off.* ELIZA *turns, sees her.*)

ELIZA. Oh, Miss James. I was going to show you that room, wasn't I? (*Crosses, seizes* LAURA'S *suitcase.*)

LAURA. Hmmmmm?

ELIZA. (*Right Center.*) I think you'll enjoy it here. It's quiet and peaceful—oh, nobody pays any mind to Mr. Gant. I'll tell you what: we don't have occurrences like this every day.

LAURA. Well, how much is it?

ELIZA. Twenty—fifteen dollars a week. Three meals a day, and the use of electricity and the bath. Do you want me to show it to you?

LAURA. No, I'm sure it will be all right.

ELIZA. (*Starting in, turns back.*) That's in advance, that is.

LAURA. (*Opens her purse, takes out a roll of one-dollar bills, puts them one by one into* ELIZA'S *outstretched hand.*) One, two, three—I always keep my money in one-dollar bills—it feels like it's more.

ELIZA. (*Almost cheerful again.*) Oh, I know what you mean. (MR. FARREL *enters by the side door with his suitcase. He is hoping to sneak out.* ELIZA *sees him as the paying business continues. Crossing to Left of* LAURA.) Mr. Farrel! Where are you going? Mr. Farrel, you've paid for a week in advance! (MR. FARREL *wordlessly gestures that it's all too much for him, exits.*) Well, they come and they go. And you're here now, isn't that nice?

LAURA. . . . Nine . . . ten. . . .

BEN. (*Enters from the other direction, hurriedly.*) I heard about Father—how is he? (*Crosses to porch.*)

ELIZA. Drunk. Dr. Maguire's taking care of him now. Ben, this is Miss James—this is my son, Ben Gant.

BEN. (*Impressed by her looks, nods.*) Miss James.

LAURA. (*Barely looking at* BEN, *nods.*) —fourteen, fifteen. There.

ELIZA. (*Puts the money in bosom of her dress.*) Thank you, dear. Miss James is going to stay with us a while, we hope! I'll take you up, dear. You'll be cozy and comfortable here. (*They start inside.*) I'll show you the rest of the house later.

LAURA. (*Turning in doorway.*) Nice to have met you, Mr. Gant. (ELIZA *and* LAURA *exit.*)

BEN. (*Imitating* LAURA's *disinterest, as he picks up cup of coffee.*) Nice to have met you, Mr. Gant. (*Shrugs, sits woodbox and lights cigarette.*)

WILL. (*Enters from the house, still sweating. Left of* BEN.) That father of yours. Do you know he kicked me? I don't want to tell you where. Why don't you watch out for him more, Ben? It's up to you boys, for your mother's sake—for Dixieland. I warned her about him—a born wanderer like he is, and a widower. But you can't advise women—not when it comes to love and sex. (*He starts off, stops Up Right.*) You might thank me for my help. No one else has.

BEN. Thank you, Uncle Will.

WILL. Bunch of ungrateful Gants. You're the only one of them who has any class. (*Exits Up Right.*)

EUGENE. (*Enters.*) Did you hear about it, Ben?

BEN. There isn't a soul in town who hasn't.

EUGENE. (*Crossing into yard.*) What's it all about? It doesn't make sense. Can you figure it out, Ben? Why does he do it?

BEN. How should I know? (*Drinks his coffee.*) Is Maguire almost through?

EUGENE. (*Hurt, not understanding* BEN's *preoccupation.*) Ben, remember in the morning when we used to walk together and you were teaching me the paper route? We talked a lot then.

BEN. Listen to him! We're talking.

EUGENE. (*Crosses, sits step.*) If he hates it so much here, why does he stay?

BEN. You stupid little fool, it's like being caught in a photograph. Your face is there, and no matter how hard you try, how are you going to step out of a photograph? (DOCTOR MAGUIRE *enters.*) Shut up now, will you. Hello, Doc. (*Rises, leaves coffee on woodbox.*)

DR. MAGUIRE. (*Entering, putting on cap.*) Your sister sure can handle that old goat like a lamb! The funny thing though is that people like him. He's a good man, when sober.

BEN. Is he all right?

DR. MAGUIRE. (*Taking bag, crossing to yard Down Right.*) He's going to be.

BEN. (*Crossing yard to Left of Down Right.*) Can I speak to you a minute about me? If you have a minute.

DR. MAGUIRE. Shoot, Ben.

BEN. (*To* EUGENE, *who has seated himself Right of door.*) Haven't you got something else to do?

. EUGENE. No.

(BEN *crosses to Right of Center table.*)

DR. MAGUIRE. (*Crossing to Right of* BEN.) What's the matter—you got pyorrhea of the toenails or is it something more private?

BEN. I'm tired of pushing daisies here. I want to push them somewhere else.

DR. MAGUIRE. What's that supposed to mean?

BEN. I suppose you've heard there's a war going on in Europe? I've decided to enlist in Canada.

EUGENE. (*Rises.*) What do you want to do that for?

BEN. (*To* EUGENE.) You keep out of this.

DR. MAGUIRE. It is a good question, Ben. Do you want to save the world? This world?

BEN. In Christ's name, Maguire, you'll recommend me, won't you? You examined me just a couple of months ago.

DR. MAGUIRE. (*Crosses, puts down his bag on Right pillar.*) Well, let's see, for a war the requirements are somewhat different. Stick out your chest. (BEN *does so; the* DOCTOR *looks him over.*) Feet? Good arch, but pigeon-toed.

BEN. Since when do you need toes to shoot a gun?

DR. MAGUIRE. (*Crossing to him.*) How're your teeth, son?

BEN. Aren't you overdoing it, Doc? (BEN *draws back his lips and shows two rows of hard white grinders. Unexpectedly* MAGUIRE *prods* BEN'S *solar plexus with a strong yellow finger and* BEN'S *distended chest collapses. He sinks to the veranda edge, coughing.*)

EUGENE. What did you do that for?

DR. MAGUIRE. (*Crosses for bag.*) They'll have to save this world without you, Ben.

BEN. (*Rises, grabs the* DOCTOR.) What do you mean?

DR. MAGUIRE. That's all. That's all.

BEN. You're saying I'm not all right?

DR. MAGUIRE. (*Turns to him.*) Who said you weren't all right?

BEN. (*Left of Down Right.*) Quit your kidding.

DR. MAGUIRE. What's the rush? We may get into this war ourselves before too long. Wait a bit. (*To* EUGENE.) Isn't that right, son? (*Turns for bag.*)

BEN. (*Grabs his Right arm.*) I want to know. Am I all right or not?

DR. MAGUIRE. Yes, Ben, you're all right. Why, you're one of the most all right people I know. (*Carefully, as he feels* BEN'S *arm.*) You're a little run down, that's all. You need some meat on those bones. (BEN *breaks from him, moves away Left.*) You can't exist with a cup of coffee in one hand and a cigarette in the other. Besides, the Altamont air is good for you. Stick around. Big breaths, Ben, big breaths. (*Picks up his bag.*)

BEN. Thanks. As a doctor, you're a fine first baseman.

DR. MAGUIRE. Take it easy. Try not to care too much. (*Exits Down Right.* BEN *puts out cigarette in coffee cup on Center table.*)

EUGENE. (*Crosses to Right of* BEN.) He's right. You should try to look after yourself more, Ben. (*Tries to comfort* BEN. BEN *avoids his touch, lurches away.*)

BEN. He doesn't have any spirit about this war, that's all that's the matter with him. (*Recovers his coffee, drinks.* EUGENE *studies him.*)

EUGENE. I didn't know you wanted to get away from here so badly.

BEN. (*Looks over at* EUGENE, *puts down coffee on Right pillar. Crosses to yard.*) Come here, you little bum. (EUGENE *approaches close.*) My God, haven't you got a clean shirt? (*He gets out some money.*) Here, take this and go get that damn long hair cut off, and get some shoes that fit, for God's sake, you look like a lousy tramp—

EUGENE. (*Backing away Left.*) Ben, I can't keep taking money from you.

BEN. What else have you got me for? (*The brothers roughhouse playfully with the money,* EUGENE *giggling. Then with sudden intense ferocity* BEN *seizes* EUGENE'S *arms, shakes him.*) You listen to me. Listen to me. You go to college, understand? Don't settle for anyone or anything—learn your lesson from me! I'm a hack on a hick paper—I'll never be anything else. You can be. Get money out of them, any way you can! Beg it, take it, steal it, but get it from them somehow. Get it and get away from them. To hell with them all! (BEN *coughs.* EUGENE *tries to help him.* BEN *escapes, sits tiredly on the veranda's edge.* EUGENE *disconsolately sinks into nearby chair Left of Center table.*) Neither Luke, nor Stevie, nor I made it. But you can, Gene. I let her hold on and hold on until it was too late. Don't let that happen to you. And Gene, don't try to please everyone— please yourself. (BEN *studies* EUGENE, *realizes his confusion and depression. Then, noticing* LAURA'S *hat which she has left on the yard table, points to it.*) Where's she from?

EUGENE. (*Follows* BEN'S *gaze to* LAURA'S *hat, picks*

it up, sniffs it.) I don't know. I don't even know her name.

BEN. Miss James. I'll have to announce her arrival in my "society" column. (*Takes hat from* EUGENE, *admires it.*) The firm young line of spring—budding, tender, virginal. "Like something swift, with wings, which hovers in a wood—among the feathery trees, suspected, but uncaught, unseen." Exquisite. (*Returns hat to table, rises.*) Want to walk downtown with me? I'll buy you a cup of mocha.

EUGENE. Maybe I ought to stay here.

BEN. (*Ruffling* EUGENE'S *hair. Crossing for coffee.*) With her around I don't blame you. I dream of elegant women myself, all the time.

EUGENE. (*Rising.*) You do? But, Ben, if you dream of elegant woman, how is it, well—

BEN. (*On porch.*) Mrs. Pert? Fatty's a happy woman—there's no pain in her she feels she has to unload onto someone else. Besides she's as adorable as a duck; don't you think so?

EUGENE. I guess you're right. I like her—myself—sure.

BEN. (*Replaces coffee cup on tray, crosses to yard Down Right.*) Some day you'll find out what it means. I've got to get back to work.

EUGENE. (*Front of Left pillar.*) Ben, I'm glad they won't take you in Canada.

BEN. (*With that upward glance.*) Listen to him! I was crazy to think of going. I have to bring you up first, don't I? (BEN *exits.*)

MISS BROWN. (*Dressed for a stroll, carrying a parasol, she enters from the house.*) Gene! You haven't even said hello to me today.

EUGENE. Hello, Miss Brown.

MISS BROWN. (*Crosses to yard Down Right.*) My, everything's quiet again. Lovely warm day, isn't it? (MISS BROWN *sings and dances sensuously for* EUGENE.)*

* "My Pony Boy" used by special permission of copyright owner, Jerry Vogel Music Co., Inc., New York 36, N. Y.

> "Pony boy, pony boy,
> Won't you be my pony boy?
> Don't say no, can't we go
> Right across the plains?"

(MISS BROWN *approaches* EUGENE, *he backs away from her stumbling against the table. She starts out through rear veranda.*)

> "Marry me, carry me—"
> "Far away with you!
> Giddy-ap, giddy-ap, giddy-ap. Oh!
> My pony boy!"

(MISS BROWN *exits.* EUGENE *sits in the yard seat, takes off one shoe and rubs his aching toes.* LAURA *enters, picks up her hat, sees* EUGENE. EUGENE *hides his shoeless foot.* MISS BROWN'S VOICE *from Offstage, receding in distance.*)

> "Pony boy, pony boy
> Mmmm, mmm, mmm—Mmmm, mmm,
>   mmm,
> Marry me, carry me
> Far away with you
> Giddy-ap, giddy-ap, giddy-ap. Oh!
> My pony boy."

(*At the door,* LAURA *looks again at* EUGENE, *smiles, exits.*)

CURTAIN

ACT ONE

SCENE 2

SCENE: *The same; that evening. The night is sensuous, warm. A light storm is threatening. Long, swaying tree shadows project themselves on the house. Seated on the side veranda are* JAKE, MRS. CLATT, FLORRY, MISS BROWN, *and* MRS. SNOWDEN. MRS. PERT *is seated in her rocker,* BEN *Left of her. They are drinking beer.* MRS. PERT *measures the socks she is knitting against* BEN'S *shoe.* JAKE CLATT *softly plays the ukulele and sings.* EUGENE *is sitting on the side door steps, lonely, yearning. Glasses of lemonade have replaced the noontime coffee cups. And a phonograph replaces the flower tray on the Up Right Center table on the porch.*

JAKE. (*Singing "K-K-Katy."*)*
        "K-K-K-aty, K-K-Katy," etc.
(*As* JAKE *finishes,* FLORRY *gently applauds.* JAKE *starts softly strumming something else.*)

MRS. PERT. (*To* BEN, *quietly.*) I know you talked to the doctor today. What did he say? Tell Fatty.

BEN. I'm out before I'm in. Oh, I know you're pleased, but you don't know how it feels to be the weakling. All the other members of this family—they're steers, mountain goats, eagles. Except Father, lately—unless he's drunk. Do you know, though, I still think of him as I thought of him as a little boy—a Titan! The house on Woodson Street that he built for Mama with his own hands, the great armloads of food he carried home—the giant fires he used to build. The woman he loved at Madame Elizabeth's. Two and three a night, I heard.

MRS. PERT. It's nice for parents to have their children think of them as they were young. (*As* BEN *chuckles.*) I mean, that's the way I'd like my children to think of me. Oh, you know what I mean.

BEN. (*Laughs with his typical glance upward.*) Listen to her!

MRS. PERT. Ben, who are you always talking to, like that? (*Imitates* BEN *looking up over his shoulder.*)

* "K-K-K-Katy," words and music by Geoffrey O'Hara © 1918, copyright renewal 1945 Leo Feist, Inc. Used by permission of the copyright owner solely for the purpose of printing in this edition. CAUTION: Permission to include this song in any performance of this play must be obtained from Leo Feist, Inc., 1540 Broadway, New York 36, N. Y.

BEN. Who, him? (*She nods.*) That's Grover, my twin. It was a habit I got into, while he was still alive.

MRS. PERT. I wish you'd known me when I was young. I was some different.

BEN. I bet you weren't half as nice and warm and round as you are now.

MRS. PERT. Ben, don't ever let your mother hear you say those things. What could she think?

BEN. Who cares what she thinks?

MRS. PERT. Dear, I only hope when the right girl comes along you won't be sorry for the affection you've lavished on me.

BEN. I don't want the "right girl." Like some more beer? I've got another bottle.

MRS. PERT. Love some more, honey.

(BEN *rises, searches under the yard table for the bottle he has hidden, realizes it's not there, suspiciously looks at* EUGENE. EUGENE *innocently gestures, then reaches behind him and tosses the beer bottle to* BEN. BEN *and* FATTY *laugh.* BEN *returns with the beer to* FATTY *as* LAURA *enters from the house.*)

JAKE. (*Rising expectantly.*) Good evening, Miss James.

LAURA. Good evening.

JAKE. Won't you sit down? (*Indicates woodbox where he has been sitting.*)

MRS. CLATT. (*As* LAURA *seems about to choose a chair.*) That's Mr. Farrel's. Yours is back there!

JAKE. (*Loudly. Moves Up Left of her.*) Mr. Farrel has left, Mother.

MRS. CLATT. What?

JAKE. Never mind. (*To* LAURA.) No sense in being formal. Won't you sing with me, Miss James?

LAURA. I love music, but I have no talent for it. (*Moves toward rear of veranda, away from the others,* JAKE *places uke on woodbox.*)

FLORRY. (*To* JAKE.) I love to sing.

(JAKE *ignores* FLORRY, *follows after* LAURA, FLORRY *tugging at* JAKE'S *coat.*)

MRS. SNOWDEN. (*To* JAKE *as he passes.*) Do you know Indiana Lullaby? It's a lovely song.

(JAKE *and* LAURA *exit.*)

BEN. I'm comfortable when I'm with you, Fatty.

MRS. PERT. That's good, so'm I.

BEN. People don't understand. Jelly roll isn't everything, is it?

MRS. PERT. Ben Gant, what kind of a vulgar phrase is that?

BEN. It's a Stumptown word. I used to deliver papers there. Sometimes those negra women don't have money to pay their bill, so they pay you in jelly roll.

MRS. PERT. Ben—your little brother's right over there listening!

BEN. (*Glances toward* EUGENE.) Gene knows all about jelly roll, don't you? Where do you think he's been all his life—in Mama's front parlor?

EUGENE. Oh, come on, Ben. (*Embarrassed laugh.*)

BEN. (*Laughs.*) There's another word I remember in the eighth grade. We had a thin, anxious-looking teacher. The boys had a poem about her. (*Quotes.*)

> "Old Miss Groody
> Has good toody."

MRS. PERT. Ben, stop it! (*They both laugh.* EUGENE *joins in.* LAURA *has managed to lose* JAKE, *has strolled around the back of the house. She enters to* EUGENE *from the side door.*)

LAURA. Good evening.

EUGENE. What!

LAURA. I said good evening.

EUGENE. (*Flustered.*) Goodyado. (*Rises, moves Down Left of her.*)

LAURA. I beg your pardon?

EUGENE. I mean—I meant to say good evening, how do you do?

LAURA. Goodyado! I like that much better. Goodyado! (*They shake hands,* LAURA *reacting to* EUGENE's *giant grip.* EUGENE *sits Left on unit.*) Don't you think that's funny?

EUGENE. It's about as funny as most things I do.

LAURA. May I sit down?

EUGENE. (*Leaping up.*) Please.

LAURA. (*As she sits.*) I'm Laura James.

EUGENE. I know. My name's Eugene Gant.

LAURA. You know, I've seen you before.

EUGENE. Yes, earlier this afternoon.

LAURA. I mean before that. I saw you throw those advertising cards in the gutter.

EUGENE. You did?

LAURA. I was coming from the station. You know where the train crosses the street? You were just standing there staring at it. I walked right by you and smiled at you. I never got such a snub before in my whole life. My, you must be crazy about trains.

EUGENE. (*Sits Left of her.*) You stood right beside me? (BEN *plays a record on the PHONOGRAPH.*) Where are you from?

LAURA. Richmond, Virginia.

EUGENE. Richmond! That's a big city, isn't it?

LAURA. It's pretty big.

EUGENE. How many people?

LAURA. Oh, about a hundred and twenty thousand, I'd say.

EUGENE. Are there a lot of pretty parks and boulevards?

LAURA. Oh, yes—

EUGENE. And fine tall buildings, with elevators?

LAURA. Yes, it's quite a metropolis.

EUGENE. Theatres and things like that?

LAURA. A lot of good shows come to Richmond. Are you interested in shows?

EUGENE. You have a big library. Did you know it has over a hundred thousand books in it?

LAURA. No, I didn't know that.

EUGENE. Well, it does. I read that somewhere. It would take a long time to read a hundred thousand books, wouldn't it?

LAURA. Yes, it would.

EUGENE. I figure about twenty years. How many books do they let you take out at one time?

LAURA. I really don't know.

EUGENE. They only let you take out two here!

LAURA. That's too bad.

EUGENE. You have some great colleges in Virginia. Did you know that William and Mary is the second oldest college in the country?

LAURA. Is it? What's the oldest?

EUGENE. Harvard! I'd like to study there! First Chapel Hill. That's our state university. Then Harvard. I'd like to study all over the world, learn all its languages. I love words, don't you?

LAURA. Yes; yes, I do.

EUGENE. Are you laughing at me?

LAURA. Of course not.

EUGENE. You are smiling a lot!

LAURA. I'm smiling because I'm enjoying myself. I like talking to you.

EUGENE. I like talking to you, too. I always talk better with older people.

LAURA. Oh!

EUGENE. They know so much more.

LAURA. Like me?

EUGENE. Yes. You're very interesting.

LAURA. Am I?

EUGENE. Oh yes! You're very interesting!

(JACK CLATT *approaches,* FLORRY MANGLE *hovering anxiously on the veranda.*)

JAKE. Miss James?

LAURA. Yes, Mr. Platt?

JAKE. Clatt.

LAURA. Clatt.

JAKE. Jake Clatt! It's a lovely evening. Would you like to take a stroll?

LAURA. It feels to me like it's going to rain.

JAKE. (*Looking at the sky.*) Oh, I don't know.

EUGENE. (*Rising, moving in between* LAURA *and* JAKE.) It's going to rain, all right.

JAKE. Oh, I wouldn't be so sure!

LAURA. Perhaps some other time, Mr. Clatt.

JAKE. Certainly. Good night, Miss James. Good night, sonny.

(EUGENE *glares after* JAKE, *who returns to the veranda under* FLORRIE'S *jealous stare. The* OTHER BOARDERS *have disappeared.* JAKE *and* FLORRY *exit.* FLORRY *hugging* JAKE'S *ukulele in her arms. Only* FATTY *and* BEN *still sit on the steps. A TRAIN WHISTLE moans mournfully in the distance.* EUGENE *cocks an ear, listens.*)

LAURA. You do like trains, don't you?

EUGENE. Mama took us on one to St. Louis to the Fair, when I was only five. Have you ever touched one?

LAURA. What?

EUGENE. A locomotive. Have you put your hand on one? You have to feel things to fully understand them.

LAURA. Aren't they rather hot?

EUGENE. Even a cold one, standing in a station yard. You know what you feel? You feel the shining steel rails under it—and the rails send a message right into your hand—a message of all the mountains that engine ever passed—all the flowing rivers, the forests, the towns, all the houses, the people, the washlines flapping in the fresh cool breeze—the beauty of the people in the way they live and the way they work—a farmer waving from his field, a kid from the school yard—the faraway places it roars through at night, places you don't even know, can hardly imagine. Do you believe it? You feel the rhythm of a whole life, a whole country clicking through your hand.

LAURA. (*Impressed.*) I'm not sure we all would. I believe *you* do.

(*There is a moment while* LAURA *looks at* EUGENE. BEN *moves up to the veranda and the phonograph plays another RECORD.* EUGENE *and* LAURA *speak simultaneously.*)

EUGENE. How long do you plan to stay here—?   LAURA. How old are you, Gene?

EUGENE. I'm sorry—please. (*Draws a chair close to* LAURA, *straddles it, facing her.*)

LAURA. No, you.

EUGENE. How long do you plan to stay here, Miss James?

LAURA. My name is Laura. I wish you'd call me that.

EUGENE. Laura. It's a lovely name. Do you know what it means?

LAURA. No.

EUGENE. I read a book once on the meaning of names. Laura is the laurel. The Greek symbol of victory.

LAURA. Victory. Maybe some day I'll live up to that! (*After a second.*) What does Eugene mean?

EUGENE. Oh, I forget.

LAURA. *You*, forget?

EUGENE. It means "well born."

LAURA. How old are you?

EUGENE. Why?

LAURA. I'm always curious about people's ages.

EUGENE. So am I. How old are you?

LAURA. I'm twenty-one. You?

EUGENE. Nineteen. Will you be staying here long?

LAURA. I don't know exactly.

EUGENE. You're only twenty-one?

LAURA. How old did you think I was?

EUGENE. Oh, about that. About twenty-one, I'd say. That's not old at all!

LAURA. (*Laughs.*) I don't feel it is!

EUGENE. I was afraid you might think I was too young for you to waste time with like this!

LAURA. I don't think nineteen is young at all!

EUGENE. It isn't, really, is it?

LAURA. (*Rises.*) Gene, if we keep rushing together like this, we're going to have a collision.

(LAURA *moves away from* EUGENE. *He follows her. They sit together on the side steps, reaching with whispers toward each other. The TURNTABLE revolves, removing* EUGENE'S *room and revealing* GANT'S *room. As it does so:*)

FATTY. Ben, what's your full name?

BEN. Benjamin Harrison Gant. Why?

FATTY. I thought Ben was short for benign.

BEN. Benign! Listen to her!

(*They laugh. The LIGHTS come up in* GANT'S *bedroom.* ELIZA, *carrying a pitcher and a glass, enters.* GANT *is in bed, turned away from her.*)

GANT. Helen?

ELIZA. (*Bitterly.*) No, it's not Helen, Mr. Gant. (*She pours a glass of water.*)

GANT. (*Without turning.*) If that's water, take it away. (*She leaves glass and pitcher on dresser.*)

ELIZA. Why aren't you asleep? Do you have any pain?

GANT. None but the everyday pain of thinking. You wouldn't know what that is.

ELIZA. I wouldn't know? (*She starts picking up* GANT'S *strewn socks and shoes.*)

GANT. How could you? You're always so busy puttering.

ELIZA. All the work I do around here, and you call it puttering?

GANT. Some people are doers, some are thinkers.

ELIZA. (*Neatly rearranging his vest on the back of the*

chair.) Somebody has to *do,* Mr. Gant. Somebody has to. Oh! I know you look on yourself as some kind of artist fella—but personally, a man who has to be brought maudlin through the streets—screaming curses—if you call that artistic!

GANT. The hell hound is at it again. Shut up, woman!

ELIZA. Mr. Gant, I came in here to see if there was something I could do for you. Only pity in my heart. Now will you please turn over and look at me when I talk to you? You know I can't stand being turned away from!

GANT. You're a bloody monster, you would drink my heart's blood!

ELIZA. You don't mean that—we've come this far together; I guess we can continue to the end. (*Picks up socks she has placed on bed.*) You know I was thinking only this morning about that first day we met. Do you realize it was thirty-one years ago, come July?

GANT. (*Groaning.*) Merciful God, thirty-one long miserable years!

ELIZA. I can remember like it was yesterday. I'd just come down from Cousin Sally's and I passed by your shop and there you were. I'll vow you looked as big as one of your tombstones—and as dusty—with a wild and dangerous look in your eye. You were romantic in those days—like the fellow says, a regular courtin' fool—"Miss Pentland," you said, "you have come into this hot and grubby shop like a cooling summer shower—like a cooling summer shower." That's just what you said!

GANT. And you've been a wet blanket ever since.

ELIZA. I forgive you your little jokes, Mr. Gant. I forgive your little jokes. (*She sits chair. Starts to fold his nightgown.*)

GANT. Do you? (*Slowly turns towards her and looks at her finally.*) Do you ever forgive me, Eliza? If I could make you understand something. I was such a strong man. I was dozing just now, dreaming of the past. The far past. The people and the place I came from. Those great barns of Pennsylvania. The order, the thrift, the plenty. It all started out so right, there. There I was a man who set out to get order and position in life. And what have I come to? Only rioting and confusion, searching and wandering. There was so much before, so much. Now it's all closing in. My God, Eliza, where has it all gone? Why am I here, now, at the rag end of my life? The years are all blotted and blurred—my youth a red waste—I've gotten old, an old man. But why here? Why here?

ELIZA. You belong here, Mr. Gant, that's why! You belong here. (*She touches his hand.*)

GANT. (*Throws away her hand.*) And as I get weaker and weaker, you get stronger and stronger!

ELIZA. (*Rise, puts folded nightgown in dresser.*) Pshaw! If you feel that way, it's because you have no position in life. If you'd ever listened to me once, things would have been different. You didn't believe me, did you, when I told you that little, old marble shop of yours would be worth a fortune some day? Will and I happened to be downtown this morning— (GANT *groans. Picks up his robe from bed.*)—and old Mr. Beecham from the bank stopped us on the street and he said, "Mrs. Gant, the bank is looking for a site to build a big new office building, and do you know the one we have our eye on?" And I said, "No." "We have our eye on Mr. Gant's shop, and we're willing to pay twenty thousand dollars for it!" Now what do you think of that? (*She sits chair, starts to mend robe.*)

GANT. And you came in here with only pity in your heart!

ELIZA. Well, I'll tell you what, twenty thousand dollars is a lot of money! Like the fellow says, "It ain't hay!"

GANT. And my angel, my Carrara angel? You were going to sell her too?

ELIZA. The angel, the angel, the angel! I'm so tired of hearing about that angel!

GANT. You always have been. Money dribbled from your honeyed lips. But never a word about my angel.

I've started twenty pieces of marble trying to capture her. But my life's work doesn't interest you.

ELIZA. If you haven't been able to do it in all these years, don't you think your gift as a stone cutter may be limited?

GANT. Yes, Mrs. Gant, it may be limited. It may be limited.

ELIZA. Then why don't you sell the shop? We can pay off the mortgage at Dixieland and then just set back big as you please and live off the income from the boarders the rest of our lives!

GANT. (*Furiously, he all but leaps from the bed.*) Oh, holy hell; Wow-ee! The boarders! That parade of incognito pimps and prostitutes, calling themselves penniless dancing masters, pining widows, part-time teachers and God knows what all! Woman, have mercy! That shop is my last refuge on earth. I beg you—let me die in peace! You won't have long to wait. You can do what you please with it after I'm gone. But give me a little comfort now. *And leave me my work!* At least my first wife understood what it meant to me. (*He sentimentally seeks the plump pillow.*) Cynthia, Cynthia . . .

ELIZA. (*Coldly.*) You promised me you would never mention her name to me again. (*There is a long silence. ELIZA bites the sewing thread, rises and tosses robe on bed.*) Mr. Gant, I guess I never will understand you. I guess that's just the way it is. Good night. Try to get some sleep. (*She tucks the bed clothes about him.*) I reckon it's like the fellow says, some people never get to understand each other—not in this life. (*Exits and stands outside GANT's door, trying to pull herself together.*)

GANT. (*Moans.*) Oh-h-h, I curse the day I was given life by that blood-thirsty monster up above. Oh-h-h, Jesus! I beg of you. I know I've been bad. Forgive me. Have mercy and pity upon me. Give me another chance in Jesus' name. . . . Oh-h-h!

(*The TURNTABLE removes GANT's room, replacing it with EUGENE's room. LIGHTS come up on the veranda.* LAURA *and* EUGENE *still sit on the side steps.* FATTY *and* BEN, *seated as earlier, are softly laughing.* ELIZA, *bitterly warped by her scene with* GANT, *enters. She starts gathering up the* BOARDERS' *lemonade glasses.*)

MRS. PERT. (*A little giddy.*) Why, if it isn't Mrs. Gant! Why don't you sit down and join us for a while?

ELIZA. (*Her sweeping glance takes in the beer glasses.*) I've told you before, Mrs. Pert, I don't tolerate drinking at Dixieland!

BEN. Oh, Mama, for God's sake—

ELIZA. You two can be heard all over the house with your carrying on.

BEN. Carrying on—listen to her!

ELIZA. (*Angrily turns off PHONOGRAPH.*) You're keeping the boarders awake.

BEN. They just went in!

ELIZA. As I came past your door just now, Mrs. Pert, there was a light under it. If you're going to spend all night out here, there's no sense in wasting electricity.

BEN. The Lord said, "Let there be light," even if it's only 40 watts.

ELIZA. Don't you get on your high horse with me, Ben Gant. You're not the one who has to pay the bills! If you did, you'd laugh out of the other side of your mouth. I don't like any such talk. You've squandered every penny you've ever earned because you've never known the value of a dollar!

BEN. The value of a dollar! (*Rises, goes into hall to get his jacket.*) Oh what the hell's the use of it, anyway? Come on, Fatty, let's go for a stroll.

FATTY. (*Rises. Crosses to yard Right of Right pillar.*) Whatever you say, Ben, old Fatty's willing.

ELIZA. (*Attacking FATTY; on step Left of her.*) I don't want any butt-ins from you, do you understand? You're just a paying boarder here. That's all. You're not a member of my family, and never will be, no matter what low methods you try!

EUGENE. (*Leaving* LAURA, *miserably.*) Mama, please.

ELIZA. (*Crosses to* EUGENE.) I'm only trying to keep decency and order here, and this is the thanks I get! You should all get down on your knees and be grateful to me!

BEN. (*Coming out of hall, slamming the screen door.*) What am I supposed to be grateful for? For what?

FATTY. (*Trying to stop it.*) Ben, Ben, come on.

BEN. (*On step Right of* ELIZA.) For selling the house that Papa built with his own hands and moving us into this drafty barn where we share our roof, our food, our pleasures, our privacy so that you can be Queen Bee? Is that what I'm supposed to be grateful for?

ELIZA. (*Picks up bottle and glasses from Left of Left pillar.*) It's that vile liquor that's talking!

EUGENE. Let's stop it! For God's sake, let's stop it! Mama, go to bed, please. Ben— (*Sees that* LAURA *has exited into the house. He frantically looks after her.*)

BEN. Look at your kid there! You've had him out on the streets since he was eight years old—collecting bottles, selling papers—anything that would bring in a penny.

ELIZA. Gene is old enough to earn his keep!

BEN. Then he's old enough for you to let go of him! But no, you'd rather hang on to him like a piece of property! Maybe he'll grow in value, you can turn a quick trade on him, make a profit on him. He isn't a son, he's an investment! You're so penny-mad that— (*Shifting the bottles and glasses into one hand,* ELIZA *slaps* BEN. *There is a long silence. They stare at each other.*) Come on, Fatty. (BEN *exits, past* FATTY, *down the street.*)

FATTY. He didn't mean it, Mrs. Gant. (*She follows* BEN.) Ben? Ben, wait for Fatty! (*Exits.*)

EUGENE. (*Quietly, miserably.*) Mama. Mama. Mama!

ELIZA. Well, she put him up to it! He never used to talk to me like that. You stood right there and saw it. Now I'll just ask you: was it my fault? Well, was it?

EUGENE. (*Looks after* LAURA.) Mama, Mama, in God's name go to bed, won't you? Just go to bed and forget about it, won't you?

ELIZA. (*Crossing porch, placing bottles, glasses on tray.*) All of you. Every single one of you. Your father, then Ben, now you—you all blame me. And not one of you has any idea, any idea—you don't know what I've had to put up with all these years.

EUGENE. Oh Mama, stop! Please stop!

ELIZA. (*Sinking onto the steps Left of Right pillar.*) I've done the best I could. I've done the best I could. Your father's never given me a moment's peace. Nobody knows what I've been through with him. Nobody knows, child, nobody knows.

EUGENE. (*Sits beside her.*) I know, Mama. I do know. Forget about it! It's all right.

ELIZA. You just can't realize. You don't know what a day like this does to me. Ben and I used to be so close— especially after little Grover died. I don't think a mother and son were ever closer. You don't remember when he was a youngster, the little notes he was always writing me. I'd find them slipped under my door, when he got up early to go on his paper route. . . . "Good morning, Mama!" . . . "Have a nice day, Mama." We were so close . . .

EUGENE. (*Gently.*) It's late. You're tired.

ELIZA. (*Managing to pull herself together.*) Well, like the fellow says, it's no use crying over *that* spilt milk. I have all those napkins and towels to iron for tomorrow.

EUGENE. (*Rises, looking toward* LAURA'S *room.*) The boarders can get along without new napkins tomorrow. Mama, why don't you get some sleep?

ELIZA. (*Rises.*) Well, I tell you what: I'm not going to spend my life slaving away here for a bunch of boarders. They needn't think it. I'm going to sit back and take things as easy as any of them. One of these days you may just find us Gants living in a big house in Doak Park. I've got the lot—the best lot out there. I made the trade with old Mr. Doak himself the other day. What about that? (*She laughs.*) He said, "Mrs. Gant, I can't trust any of my agents with you. If I'm to make anything on this deal, I've got to look out. You're the sharpest trader in this town!" "Why, pshaw, Mr. Doak," I said, (I never let on I believed him or anything), "all I want is a fair return on my investment. I believe in everyone making his profit and giving the other fellow a chance. Keep the ball a-rolling," I said, laughing as big as you please! (*She laughs again in recollection.*) "You're the sharpest trader in this town." That's exactly his words. Oh, dear— (EUGENE *joins her laughter.*) Well—I'd better get at those napkins. Are you coming in, child?

EUGENE. (*Rises, looks toward* LAURA'S *room.*) In a little while.

ELIZA. Don't forget to turn off the sign. Good night, son. (EUGENE *returns to* ELIZA. *She kisses him.*) Get a *good* night's sleep, boy. You mustn't neglect your health. (*She starts in.*)

EUGENE. Don't work too late. (*Starts toward the side door.*)

ELIZA. Gene, you know where Sunset Terrace runs up the hill? At the top of the rise? Right above Dick Webster's place. That's my lot. You know where I mean, don't you?

EUGENE. Yes, Mama.

ELIZA. And that's where we'll build—right on the very top. I tell you what, though, in another five years that lot'll bring twice the value. You mark my words!

EUGENE. Yes, Mama. Now, for God's sake, go and finish your work so you can get to sleep!

ELIZA. No sir, they needn't think I'm going to slave away all my life. I've got plans, same as the next fellow! You'll see. (*Offstage, the church CHIMES start to sound the midnight hour.*) Well, good night, son.

EUGENE. Good night, Mama. . . . (ELIZA *exits.* EUGENE *calls with desperate softness.*) Laura—Laura! (*Gives up, turns away.* LAURA *enters through the side door.* EUGENE *turns, sees her.*) Did you hear all that? I'm sorry, Laura.

LAURA. What's there to be sorry about?

EUGENE. Would you like to take a walk?

LAURA. It's a lovely evening.

EUGENE. It might rain.
LAURA. I love the rain.

(EUGENE *and* LAURA *hold out their hands to each other.*
EUGENE approaches her, takes her hand. They go off
together D. L. *For a moment the stage is silent.*
ELIZA enters with an envelope in her hand.)

ELIZA. See, looky here—I made a map of it. Sunset
Terrace goes— (*She looks around.*) Gene? Eugene? (*She*
looks up towards EUGENE'S *room.*) Gene, I asked you to
turn out the sign! That boy. I don't know what I'm going
to do with him. (*Goes into the hall, turns out the SIGN*
and stands for a moment. Offstage, a passerby is whistling
"Genevieve." ELIZA *comes down to the edge of the ve-*
randa and looks out into the night in the direction taken
by BEN *and* FATTY.) Ben? Ben?

SLOW CURTAIN

ACT TWO

Scene 1

Scene: Gant's *marble yard and shop, a week later.
Under a high, wide shed is the sign: W. O. GANT—
STONE CARVER. The shed is on a back street,
behind the town square. In the distance can be seen
the outline of Dixieland. Inside the shed, are slabs
of marble and granite and some finished monuments
—an urn, a couchant lamb and several angels. The
largest and most prominent monument is a delicately
carved angel of a lustrous white Carrara marble,
with an especially beautiful smiling countenance.
There is a cutting area Down Right, protected from
the sun by a shade, where* Eugene, *wearing one of
his father's aprons, is discovered operating a pedalled
emery wheel. At the other side of the shed is an office with a grimy desk, a telephone, and a curtain
into another room beyond. A sidewalk runs between
the shed and a picket fence Upstage. Near the office is a stone seat, bearing the inscription, "Rest
here in peace."* Eliza *enters from the street Right.
The prim shabbiness of her dress is in contrast to
her energetic mood and walk.*

Eliza. (*Crosses to office, calls inside.*) Mr. Gant! Mr.
Gant!

Eugene. (*Stops wheel, calls.*) Papa's not here now,
Mama.

Eliza. (*Approaches* Eugene *just as he accidentally
blows some marble dust in her face.*) Where is he? Gene,
you know I can't stand that marble dust—will you step
out here where I can talk to you? Besides, I can't stand
not to see the fact I'm talking to. My goodness, spruce up,
boy—how many times do I have to tell you? Shoulders
back—like you *are* somebody. And smile, look pleasant.

46

(EUGENE *gives that idiotic grin.* ELIZA *indicates Laughran is Off Up Left.*) O pshaw! I hope your father's not over at you-know-where again.

EUGENE. He went to buy a newspaper for the obituaries.

ELIZA. How enterprising of him! But he won't follow up on it. Oh no, he says it's ghoulish to contact the bereaved ones right off. I declare, tombstones are no business anyway, any more—in this day and age people die too slowly. (EUGENE *crosses with stencil letter and chalk to Left of Center table.* ELIZA *sinks onto stone seat, leans back; for a brief instant seems actually to rest.*) I tell you what, this feels good. I wish I had as much time as some folks and could sit outside and enjoy the air. (*Notices* EUGENE *looking at her dress, as he works lettering a marble slab.*) What are you looking at? I don't have a rent, do I?

EUGENE. I was just noticing you have on your dealing and bargaining costume again.

ELIZA. Eugene Gant, whatever do you mean by that? Don't I look all right? Heaven knows, I always try to look neatly respectable.

EUGENE. (*Crosses to Right unit for chalk.*) Come on, Mama.

ELIZA. What! I declare! I might have a better dress than this, but law's sake, there's some places it don't pay to advertise it! Oh, Gene, you're smart, smart, I tell you! You've got a future ahead of you, child.

EUGENE. (*Crossing to Left of Center table.*) Mama, what kind of a future have I got if I can't get an education?

ELIZA. Pshaw, boy, you'll get your education if my plans work out! I'll tell you what, though—in the meantime, it wouldn't hurt you to work in Uncle Will's office, would it?

EUGENE. (*Working.*) I don't know anything about real estate, Mama.

ELIZA. What do you have to know? Buying and selling is an instinct, and you've got it. You've got my eye for looking and seeing and remembering, and that's what's important. Why there isn't a vital statistic about a soul in Altamont I don't carry right in my head. What they make, what they owe—what they're hiding, what they show! (GENE *crosses to Right unit for stencil letter and then back to Center table. She laughs, enjoying her cleverness.*) You see, Eugene, I'm a poet, too—"a poet and I don't know it, but my feet show it—they're longfellows!" (*She leans back, chuckles.*) Oh dear, I can't get a smile out of you this morning. You've been so strange all this last week. (*Rises, slaps him on his back.*) Gene, stand with your shoulders back. If you go humped over, you'll get lung trouble sure as you're born. (*Moves Upstage, looks toward the town center where she presumes* GANT *is.*) That's one thing about your papa: he always carried himself straight as a rod. Of course, he's not as straight now as he used to be—Gene, *what* in the world are you standing on one foot and then the other for? Do you have to go to the bathroom?

EUGENE. Mama! Asking me that at my age!

ELIZA. Then why are you fidgeting? It's not often we have a nice chance to chat like this.

EUGENE. Papa's paying me thirty cents an hour!

ELIZA. Paying you? How did you manage that?

EUGENE. I told him I needed the money.

ELIZA. For heaven's sake, what for? You've got your room and board.

EUGENE. Don't you think I need new clothes for one thing?

ELIZA. Pshaw! The way you're still growing? It doesn't pay. (EUGENE *returns to work. She purses her lips, looks at him significantly.*) Has my baby gone and got himself a girl?

EUGENE. (*Exasperated, sits on table.*) What of it? What if it were true? Haven't I as much right as anyone?

ELIZA. Pshaw! You're too young to think of girls, especially that Miss James. She's practically a mature woman compared to you. I don't think you realize how young you are, just because you're tall and read a lot of books.

(*Sounds of CAR off Right.* ELIZA *looks off.*) Pshaw!
That's your Uncle Will come for me. Say, how long does
it take your father to buy a newspaper, anyway?

EUGENE. He said he'd be right back. Is it something
important?

ELIZA. (*Crosses for purse and stole she has left on
bench.*) Oh, I've got plans, Gene, plans for him, plans for
all of us. Well, tell him I'll be back. Second thought,
don't tell him, I'll just catch him. I want you to be here,
too. Work hard, child!

(ELIZA *exits, the CAR leaves.* EUGENE *approaches the
Carrara angel, touches the draped folds over her
breast.* GANT *enters Upper Left, watches smiling. He
has had a few beers, but he is not drunk.* EUGENE *becomes aware of* GANT'S *presence, starts guiltily.
Crosses Down Right.*)

GANT. (*Crossing to angel.*) I've done that myself many
a time, son. Many a time. Well, what did your mother
have to say?

EUGENE. Did you see her?

GANT. (*Crossing to unit Left for apron.*) I've been
sitting over at Laughran's waiting for her to leave. What
a long-winded bag!

EUGENE. You promised the doctor you wouldn't go to
Laughran's.

GANT. (*Putting on his apron.*) What difference does it
make? A couple of beers won't hurt what I've got. Was
that Will Pentland she went off with?

EUGENE. Yes.

GANT. *Upper Left Center.* Aha! And she said she's be
back?

EUGENE. Yes.

GANT. I have a mind what she's up to. She'll be back
with freshly drawn-up papers tucked in her bosom. Yes,
when you touch the breast of Miss Eliza, you feel the
sharp crackle of bills of sale—(*Crosses to angel.*) not like
the bosom of this angel. She begins to look better after a

bath, doesn't she? I've been neglecting her lately. My, how she gleams!

EUGENE. (*Sits below angel.*) Papa, you were young when you got married, weren't you?

GANT. What?

EUGENE. When did you get married?

GANT. (*Crossing to Left of Center table to work.*) It was thirty-one bitter years ago when your mother first came wriggling around that corner at me like a snake on her belly—

EUGENE. I don't mean Mama. How old were you when you were first married? To Cynthia?

GANT. By God, you better not let your mother hear you say that name!

EUGENE. I want to know—how old were you?

GANT. (*Crossing Down Right Center.*) Well, I must have been twenty-eight. Ah, Cynthia, Cynthia!

EUGENE. You loved her, didn't you, Papa?

GANT. She had a real glowing beauty. Sweet, noble, proud, and yet soft, soft—she died in her bloom.

EUGENE. She was older than you, wasn't she?

GANT. Yes. Ten years.

EUGENE. Ten years! But it didn't make any difference, did it?

GANT. (*Confidingly.*) She was a skinny, mean, tubercular old hag who nearly drove me out of my mind! (*Crosses to Center table to work.*)

EUGENE. (*Shocked.*) Then why do you talk about her the way you do? To Mama?

GANT. Because I'm a bastard, Gene. I'm a bastard! (LAURA *enters Upper Right carrying a picnic basket, her mood somewhat restless.*) Say, isn't this a pretty little somebody looking for you?

EUGENE. (*Crosses to her.*) Laura!

LARUA. (*Left of* GANT.) Hello, Mr. Gant.

GANT. Hello!

LAURA. (*Crossing to Right of angel.*) Hello, Gene. So this is your shop?

GANT. (*A step toward her.*) This is a real pleasure.

It's not often I see *smiling* people around here. Haven't you got fed up with our little resort, young lady?

LAURA. I'm really just beginning to enjoy it here.

GANT. What do you find to enjoy about it?

LAURA. Oh, the countryside is beautiful. Gene and I have had lots of pleasant walks in the hills.

GANT. Oh, so it's Gene who makes it pleasant for you, hey?

EUGENE. Come on, Papa! Hah, hah— (*Embarrassed laugh and turns away.*)

GANT. You're fond of Gene, aren't you?

LAURA. He's very nice and intelligent.

GANT. Gene's a good boy—our best.

LAURA. (*Looking around.*) My, isn't this shop interesting? How did you happen to become a stone-cutter, Mr. Gant?

(EUGENE *puts apron on bench, studies* LAURA *during this, sensing her evasiveness to him.*)

GANT. Well, I guess you'd call it a passion with some people. When I was a boy Gene's age, I happened to pass a shop something like this. (*Of the angel.*) And this very angel was there. She's Carrara marble—(*Sits Right on Center table.*) from Italy. And as I looked at her smiling face, I felt, more than anything in the world, I wanted to carve delicately with a chisel. It was as though, if I could do that, I could bring something of me out onto a piece of marble. Oh, the reminiscences of the old always bore the young.

LAURA. No, they don't.

GANT. So I walked into that shop, and asked the stone-cutter if I could become an apprentice. Well, I worked there for five years. When I left, I bought the angel. (*He looks at the angel with longing.*) I've hardly had her out of my sight, since I bet I've started twenty pieces of marble, but I've never been able to capture her. . . . I guess there's no use trying any more— (*He becomes silent, morose. Sensitively* EUGENE *touches* GANT'S *shoulder, looks at* LAURA.)

EUGENE. Would you like to look around, Laura?

LAURA. I'm afraid I'm bothering you at your work.

GANT. (*Looks at* EUGENE, *coming out of his distant thought and mood.*) No, no. Show her about, Gene. (*Suddenly, decisive.*) I have some other things I must do— (*Starts toward office, pauses.*)—though some people find looking at tombstones depressing. Still we all come to them in the end. (GANT *exits.*)

EUGENE. Why do you think you might be bothering me?

LAURA. You are supposed to be working.

EUGENE. (*A step to her.*) You came here to see me. What's happened, Laura? Something's different today.

LAURA. (*Crossing Left, puts picnic basket on marble slab Down Right.*) Oh, don't pay any attention to me. I just—I don't know.

EUGENE. What's in the basket?

LAURA. I asked Helen to pack us a picnic lunch.

EUGENE. (*Crosses for basket and takes her hand.*) Good! Let's go!

LAURA. (*Pulling away.*) Not now.

EUGENE. (*Puts his arm around her.*) What is it, Laura? What's the matter? Have I done something wrong?

LAURA. (*Shakes her head.*) Gene, Helen knows about us! And your father too. He—

EUGENE. I don't care—I want the whole world to know. (*Picks up basket.*) Here, let's go.

LAURA. (*Pulling away.*) No. Let's not talk about it. (*Sits on stool, near slab.*) This is pretty marble. Where's it from?

EUGENE. Laura, you don't give a damn where that marble came from!

LAURA. (*Starts to cry.*) Oh, Gene, I'm so ashamed, so ashamed.

EUGENE. (*Sits beside her on slab.*) Laura, my darling, what is it?

LAURA. Gene, I lied to you—I'm twenty-three years old.

EUGENE. Is that all?

LAURA. You're not nineteen either. You're seventeen.

EUGENE. I'm a thousand years old, all the love I've stored up for you. (*Again puts his arms around her.*)

LAURA. (*Struggling away.*) I'm an older woman—

EUGENE. In God's name, what does that have to do with us?

LAURA. There have to be rules!

EUGENE. Rules are made by jealous people. They make rules to love by so even those with no talent for it can at least pretend. We don't need rules. We don't have to pretend. Oh, Laura, my sweet, what we have is so beautiful, so rare . . . how often in life can you find it?

LAURA. (*Escaping his arms, rises, crosses Down Right Center and turns to him.*) Eugene, you're a young boy, a whole world just waiting for you.

EUGENE. You are my world, Laura. You always will be. Don't let anything destroy us. Don't leave me alone. I've always been alone.

LAURA. It's what you want, dear. It's what you'll always want. You couldn't stand anything else. You'd get so tired of me. You'll forget—you'll forget.

EUGENE. I'll never forget. I won't live long enough. (*Takes her in his arms, kisses her.*) Will you forget?

LAURA. (*As he holds her.*) Oh my darling, every word, every touch, how could I?

EUGENE Then nothing has changed. Has it? Has it?

MADAME ELIZABETH'S VOICE. (*Off.*) Good morning! (MADAME ELIZABETH, *38, the town madame, enters along the street Upper Left. She is well-clad, carries herself stylishly. She sees* EUGENE *and* LAURA, *stops as they break from each other.*)

EUGENE. Good morning, Madame Elizabeth.

MADAME ELIZABETH. (*Closing her parasol.*) Is Mr. Gant here?

EUGENE. He's inside.

MADAME ELIZABETH. Well, don't let me keep you from

what you're doing. (*Approaches office, calls.*) Mr. Gant!
(*Places parasol Down Left of bench. Crosses to angel.*)

(LAURA *and* EUGENE *exit into yard Down Right.* GENE
carrying off Down Right stool. GANT, *changed into
another, better pair of trousers, tying his tie, enters.*)

GANT. Elizabeth, my dear Elizabeth! Well, this is a
surprise! (*Seizes her hands.*)

MADAME ELIZABETH. (*Sentimentally looking him over.*)
Six years, W.O. Six years—except to nod to. Time, what a
thief you are.

GANT. He hasn't stolen from you—you're still as hand-
some and stylish as ever. Won't you sit down?

MADAME ELIZABETH. (*Crossing to bench Down Left
Center.*) Oh, W.O.—you and your gallant manners. But
I'm no chicken any more, and no one knows it better than
I do. If you only knew how often we talk about you up
on Eagle Crescent. What a man you were! Wild! Bacchus
himself. You remember the song you used to sing?

GANT. Life was many songs in those days, Elizabeth.

MADAME ELIZABETH. But when you got liquored up
enough—don't you remember? Of course I can't boom it
out like you do. (*Sings, imitating* GANT. GANT *joins her.*)

> "Up in that back room, boys,
> Up in *that* back room
> All those kisses and those hugs
> Among the fleas and bugs
> In the evening's gloom, boys,
> I pity your sad doom.
> Up in that back room, boys,
> Up in *that* back room."

(*Both laugh.* GANT *gives her an affectionate fanny slap.*)

GANT. The loss of all that, that's the worst, Elizabeth.

MADAME ELIZABETH. (*Sitting on the bench Downstage.*) Oh, W.O., W.O.! We do miss you.

GANT. (*Joining her on the bench.*) How are all the
girls, Elizabeth?

MADAME ELIZABETH. (*Suddenly distressed.*) That's what I came to see you about. I lost one of them last night. (*Takes handkerchief from her pocket, quietly cries into it.*)

GANT. Oh. I'm sorry to hear that.

MADAME ELIZABETH. Sick only three days. I'd have done anything in the world for her. A doctor and two trained nurses by her all the time.

GANT. Too bad. Too bad. Which one was it?

MADAME ELIZABETH. Since your time, W.O. We called her Lily.

GANT. Tch—tch—tch! Lily.

MADAME ELIZABETH. I couldn't have loved her more if she had been my own daughter. Twenty-two. A child, a mere child. And not a relative who would do anything for her. Her mother died when she was thirteen, and her father is a mean old bastard who wouldn't even come to her death-bed.

GANT. He will be punished.

MADAME ELIZABETH. As sure as there's a God in heaven—the old bastard! I hope he rots! Such a fine girl, such a bright future for her. She had more opportunities than I ever had—and you know what I've done here. I'm a rich woman today, W.O. Why, not even your wife owns more property than I do. I beg your pardon—I hope you don't mind my speaking of her— (GANT *gestures to go right ahead.*) Mrs. Gant and I both understand that property is what makes a person hold one's head up! And Lily could have had all that too. Poor Lily! No one knows how much I'll miss her. (*A moment's quiet.* GANT *is respecting her grief.*)

GANT. There! There! (*As he comfortingly pats her hand.*) I suppose you'll be wanting something for her grave? (*As* MADAME ELIZABETH *nods, he rises, crossing to Left of lamb.*) Here's a sweet lamb—*couchant* lamb, it's called. "Couchant" means lying-down in French. That should be appropriate.

MADAME ELIZABETH. No, I've already made up my

mind— (*Rises, moves toward the Carrara angel.*) I want that angel.

GANT. (*Crosses to Left of her.*) You don't want *her,* Elizabeth. Why, she's a white elephant. Nobody can afford to buy her!

MADAME ELIZABETH. I can and I want her.

GANT. (*Crossing Right.*) My dear Elizabeth, I have other fine angels. What about this one? My own carving.

MADAME ELIZABETH. No. Ever since I first saw that angel, I thought, when somebody who means something to me goes, she's going to be on the grave.

GANT. That angel's not for sale, Elizabeth.

MADAME ELIZABETH. Then why should you have her out here?

GANT. The truth is, I've promised her to someone.

MADAME ELIZABETH. (*Crossing to bench for her purse then back to angel.*) I'll buy her from whoever you promised and give them a profit. Cash on the line. Who did you sell it to?

GANT. (*Crossing to Right of her with urn.*) My dear Madame Elizabeth, here is a nice expensive Egyptian urn. Your beloved Lily would like that.

MADAME ELIZABETH. Egyptian urns—pah! Pee pots! I want the angel!

GANT. (*With growing intensity, angrily replaces urn on unit.*) It's not for sale! Anything you like—*everything* you like—I'll give it to you—I'll make you a present, for old times' sake. But not my angel!

MADAME ELIZABETH. Now, let's not waste any more time over this. How much, W.O.?

GANT. She's Carrara marble from Italy, and too good for any whore! (*He calls.*) Eugene—Eugene!

MADAME ELIZABETH. (*Furious.*) Why you old libertine, how dare you speak to me like that?

EUGENE. (*Entering, with* LAURA.) What is it, Father? What's the matter?

MADAME ELIZABETH. Your father's a stubborn old nut, that's what!

GANT. (*Crosses toward office, turns.*) I'm sorry if I've offended you.

MADAME ELIZABETH. You have, W.O., deeply!

GANT. Gene, will you be so kind and see if you can wait upon the Madame? (*Exits into the inner room of the office.*)

MADAME ELIZABETH. (*Crossing Left.*) I've heard the trouble your mother has with the old terror—now I believe it! All I'm asking is that he sells me that angel— for one of my dear girls who's gone—a dear, young girl in the flower of her life—(*Of* LAURA.) like this young girl here—

EUGENE. (*Upper Center.*) Madame Elizabeth, I believe Papa is saving that angel for his own grave.

MADAME ELIZABETH. (*Sits on bench.*) Oh-h-h, why didn't he say so? Why didn't he tell me? Poor, poor W.O. Well, of course in that case— (*She partially recovers; to* LAURA.) If you were to think of *your* death, dear—if you can, I mean, and we never know, we never know—is there something here that would appeal to you?

LAURA. (*Crosses to Right of Center table. Looks around.*) I like the little lamb.

MADAME ELIZABETH. Lambs are for children, aren't they?

EUGENE. (*Stoops Left of lamb.*) Lambs are for anybody. Put your hand on it. Feel it. (MADAME ELIZABETH'S *hand strokes across the lamb.*) Isn't it cool and content and restful? And you could have a poem engraved on the base.

MADAME ELIZABETH. A poem—

EUGENE. Let's see if we can find something you'd like. (*Picks up book from desk.*) Here's a book of Fifty Fine Memorial Poems. (MADAME ELIZABETH *still strokes the lamb;* EUGENE *finds a poem.*) See if you like this— (*Reads.*)

"She went away in beauty's flower,
    Before her youth was spent;
    Ere life and love had lived their hour,
    God called her—and she went."

(MADAME ELIZABETH *sobs.*)
"Yet whispers faith upon the wind;
No grief to her was given.
She left your love and went to find
A greater one in heaven."

MADAME ELIZABETH. (*Quoting, through her heartfelt tears.*) "She left *your* love and went to find
A greater one in heaven. . . ."
(*Rises, addresses* EUGENE.) I hope you never lose some-one you love, boy. (*Gets parasol.*) Well, let me know when the little lying-down lamb is ready. (*She nods with majestic dignity to* LAURA, *exits.* WILL *and* ELIZA *enter, look off in the direction taken by* MADAME ELIZABETH.)

ELIZA. Don't stare after her, Will! You know who that is. (*To* EUGENE.) Was that shameless woman here to see your father?

EUGENE. One of the girls at Eagle Crescent died. She bought a monument.

ELIZA. Oh she did! She bought one! Well, your father certainly has to deal with all kinds of people. Will, go in and tell Mr. Gant that we're here. (WILL *exits.* ELIZA *looks at* LAURA.) Oh, Miss James, it's five minutes to dinner time at Dixieland, and you know the rules about being late.

EUGENE. (*Crosses to pick up basket.*) Laura and I are going on a picnic.

ELIZA. Not now, you're not. (*To* LAURA.) My dear, I want to talk privately to Mr. Gant—to Eugene, too, and I've asked Ben to join us.

EUGENE. We've made plans, Mama.

ELIZA. (*Beside bench.*) Son, this is a family conference.

LAURA. Gene, please—I'll wait for you over at Wood-ruff's. Please. (LAURA *and* EUGENE *stroll off Up Right whispering.* WILL *enters from office paring his nails.*)

ELIZA. Is he in there?

WILL. He's there. We've got him cornered. (*They chuckle.* BEN, *looking feverish and ill, enters Up Left.*)

BEN. Hello, Uncle Will. Hello, Mama—you look like

you just swallowed fifty or a hundred acres. What did you buy today?

ELIZA. Now, Ben, it just happens that today we're selling—I hope we are, anyway.

BEN. What's it all about?

ELIZA. (*Crossing to Center.*) You just sit down there. I may not need you, but I want you to be here.

BEN. (*Sits beneath the angel.*) I hope it won't take long.

GANT. (*Enters. He wears a coat of carefully brushed black wool, a tie, and carries his hat which he leaves just inside the office.*) Good morning, Miss Eliza.

ELIZA. My, how elegant! Aren't we burning a river this morning?

GANT. (*Places hat on office stool, crosses to Left of Center table.*) I heard you were out here, Miss Eliza. I so seldom have a visit from you! (*He gestures the tribute.*)

ELIZA. That's most gracious. You may all sit down now. Gene! Will! (EUGENE *enters, sits on Center table.* WILL *sits on office step.* GANT *moves a chair to Center.*) Now, Mr. Gant—

GANT. (*As he places chair Left of Center table and sits.*) This isn't one of your temperance meetings?

ELIZA. (*A bit surprised. Putting stole and purse on bench.*) Our private temperance problem—that's a part of it, yes. Mr. Gant, how old are you?

GANT. I've lost track.

ELIZA. You're sixty years old in December. And if Dr. Maguire were here, he could tell you—

GANT. I've heard what Doc Maguire has to tell me. I shouldn't be lifting these marbles. I shouldn't be drinking liquor. I should take a nice long rest.

ELIZA. Then you save me a great deal of argument about that. Now, Gene— (*Crosses over to* EUGENE *above Center table.*)

EUGENE. Yes, Mama? (*Rises.*)

ELIZA. You want to go to college, don't you?

EUGENE. Very much.

ELIZA. Well, I figure that four years at Chapel Hill

will cost thirty-four hundred dollars—but of course you'll have to wait on table. Otherwise it would be forty-four hundred dollars, which is ridiculous—at the moment we don't even have thirty-four hundred dollars—

GANT. Oh, for God's sake, get to the point, Miss Eliza. Have you got the papers from the bank?

ELIZA. (*Crosses to Left of him.*) Why, what do you mean, what papers?

GANT. You know what I mean. Fish for them, woman! (*Pointing to her bosom.*) *Go ahead, fish for them.* (ELIZA *turns her back, from her bosom fishes out a large envelope.* GANT *laughs, a roaring bitter laugh, leaps up to* EUGENE *who joins the laughter.*)

ELIZA. (*Angrily.*) What in the world are you two hyenas laughing at?

GANT. Oh, as you would say, Miss Eliza, that's a good one, that's a *good* one.

ELIZA. Well, I am glad to see you in a *good* mood.

GANT. (*Crossing Down Right Center.*) So the bank wants this little old lot, here? That's what you told me, didn't you? Though I can't for the life of me see why.

WILL. There's a new business street going through here in a few months.

GANT. (*Crosses to Right of her.*) Let me see the check.

ELIZA. (*Takes check from envelope, hands it to him.*) Well, it's for twenty thousand dollars. Will had to guarantee it personally for me to bring it here. Did you ever see anything like it? Two, zero, coma, zero—zero—zero—decimal—zero—zero!

GANT. "W. O. Gant." It seems to be in good order, all right.

ELIZA. Well—it is—and Will's looked over this deed, and it's all in order too, isn't it, Will? (*Hands the deed to* GANT.) Give me your pen, Will.

WILL. (*Hands* ELIZA *the pen.*) And I just had it filled.

GANT. (*Examining the deed. Crosses, sits Center.*) This fine print—I really do need glasses.

ELIZA. You can trust Will. (*Puts pen on work table.*) He's been all over it, Mr. Gant!

WILL. (*Looks at angel.*) What about the marble stock and the monuments?

ELIZA. They're not included.

EUGENE. Papa—the years you've spent here—all your fine work. Please don't give it up.

ELIZA. Now, Gene, your father knows what he's doing.

EUGENE. But he's such a fine stonecutter!

GANT. You think my work is fine, son?

EUGENE. Isn't it, Ben? (GANT *crosses down right into the marble yard, looking about.*)

ELIZA. Your father knows his duty to all of us—and to himself—

EUGENE. There isn't a cemetery in the state that isn't filled with his work—you can always recognize it. Clean, and pure and beautiful. Why should he give it up?

ELIZA. Why, law, I don't say he should give it up entirely. He can have another little shop further out of town!

EUGENE. But he's too old to transplant now, Mama. This is his street. Everyone knows him here. People pass by. Mr. Jannadeau's shop next door, and Woodruff's across the way—All the people and places Papa knows!

GANT. And Tim Laughran's down the block!

ELIZA. (*Crosses down to* GANT.) Oh, yes. That's another reason for getting rid of this place. Put yourself out of temptation's way, Mr. Gant.

GANT. (*Sits on slab.*) I certainly do love it here.

EUGENE. Don't give it up, Papa.

BEN. What do you want to do to him, Mama?

ELIZA. Now, looky here—you are a fine stone cutter—why, haven't I always said so? But it's time you rested. You want to live a long time, don't you? (*Sits beside him on slab.*)

GANT. Well, sometimes, I'm not sure.

ELIZA. Well, you do—and I want you to live a long time—we all want to! People can talk about a short but sweet life, but we all want to live! Look at me, I'm fifty-seven years old. I've borne nine children, raised six of them, and worked hard all my life. I'd like to back up and rest a little myself. And we can, Mr. Gant. If you'll just sign that little slip of paper. I guarantee, in a year from now, you'll have completely forgotten this dingy, crooked, dusty yard. Won't he, Ben? Won't he? Ben!

BEN. Some people have trouble forgetting some things, Mama.

ELIZA. Why, pshaw, I'm going to *see* to it that he forgets it. I'll have time to look after you. Won't I, Mr. Gant?

GANT. You're right about one thing, Miss Eliza—that I can't dispute. You have worked hard. (*Rises, moves to Center work table.*)

EUGENE. Papa, please, don't do it. (GANT *sits at work table, signs the deed.* ELIZA *crosses to him, picks it up.*)

ELIZA. Thank you, Mr. Gant. Now the check. You know what I'm going to do? I'm going to plan a great, glorious celebration. (*Gives the deed to* WILL, *speaks to* EUGENE.) We'll ask your brother Luke to come home, if the Navy will let him out. And we'll invite Stevie, and Daisy and her husband, too, except if she brings those whiny children of hers. (*Notices* GANT *just looking at the check.*) Turn it over, Mr. Gant. Sign it on the back.

GANT. Why do I have to sign it?

ELIZA. Endorse it, that's all. "W. O. Gant," like it's written on the front of the check.

GANT. That can wait until I offer it, can't it?

ELIZA. To clear the check, Mr. Gant!

GANT. I'm not used to these things. How do you clear it?

ELIZA. You sign it—I'll deposit it in the Dixieland account, then we draw checks on it.

GANT. We?

ELIZA. Yes. You draw what you want. I'll draw what we need for Gene's college—for Dixieland, and for anything else we need.

GANT. (*Rises, crosses to office.*) I think I'll wait to cash it until I get to Chapel Hill. The bank has a branch there, doesn't it, Will? (*Gives* WILL *his pen.*)

ELIZA. Why would you want to cash it in Chapel Hill?

GANT. This is my check, isn't it? I'm the one who had the foresight to buy this little pie-cornered lot thirty-one years ago for four hundred dollars—money from the estate of Cynthia L. Gant, deceased. I guess I'm entitled to the profit.

ELIZA. Now, Mr. Gant, if you're thinking to get my dander up!

GANT. (*Picks up hat, puts it on.*) Miss Eliza, I've been wanting to get away from here for a long time. I'm taking Gene with me. (*Crosses to* EUGENE.) I'm going to put him in that college there at Chapel Hill.

EUGENE. Now?

GANT. Now! And then I'm going to travel—and when Gene's free in the summer, we'll travel together. (*Crosses back to* ELIZA.) And there's nothing in this whole wide world that you're going to do to stop me. And I can just see the word Dixieland forming on your cursed lips. What about Dixieland? Nothing for Dixieland? *No, not one god-damn red cent!* You've plenty of property of your own you can sell. If it's rest and comfort you really want, sell it, woman, sell it! But I think you like working hard, because then that makes us all feel sorry for you. And I do feel sorry for you too, from the bottom of my heart. (*Puts check in pocket.*) Well, Eugene!

EUGENE. Papa, I can't go now.

GANT. Why not? You haven't got any better clothes . . . so you might as well go as you are. I guess we'll say our good-byes. (*Addresses the angel.*) So long, dear Carrara angel. I'll arrange for us to be together again some day. Good-bye, Ben— Tell Helen—tell Helen I'll write to her. (*Shakes hands with* BEN.)

ELIZA. (*Leaping at* GANT.) I won't let you do this. I won't let you.

EUGENE. MAMA!

ELIZA. (*Seizes check from* GANT'S *pocket, tears it up, flings it on the ground.*) All right, all right, all right! There's your check. I guess there's nothing to prevent you from going to the bank and trying to get another check, but it won't work because I'm going to put an

injunction against you. I'll prove you're not responsible
to sell this property, or even to own it. I'll get guardian-
ship over you! Everyone knows the times you've been to
the cure—the threats you've made to me—the times
you've tried to kill me—I'll tell them. You're a madman,
Mr. Gant, a madman. You're not going to get away with
this. I'll fight you tooth and nail, tooth and nail. And
I'll win. (*Trembling, she picks up her handbag from the
stone seat.*)

GANT. All the things you've said about me are true,
Eliza. I've only brought you pain. Why don't you let me
go?

ELIZA. Because you're my husband, Mr. Gant! You're
my husband. Thirty-one years together and we'll go on—
we must go on. A house divided against itself cannot
stand. We must try to understand and love each other.
We must try. . . . (*Exits Up Right.*)

GANT. (*Quietly.*) Take her home, will you, Will?
(WILL *hurries after* ELIZA. *A long moment.* BEN, *weak
and feverish, dries his forehead with his handkerchief.*
GANT *sinks into a chair.*) Eugene, go over to Laughran's
and get me a bottle. You heard me.

EUGENE. No, Papa.

GANT. Are you still paddling along after your mother?

BEN. Leave Gene alone. If you want to get sick, do it
yourself.

GANT. Ungrateful sons! Oh, the sad waste of years, the
red wound of all our mistakes. (*Rises, exits Up Left.*
EUGENE *looks after him.*)

BEN. The fallen Titan. He might have succeeded if
he hadn't tried to take you. He could still make it, but
he won't try again.

EUGENE. They loved each other once. They must have
had one moment in time that was perfect. What happened? It frightens me, Ben; how can something so
perfect turn into this torture?

BEN. They're strangers. They don't know each other.
No one ever really comes to know anyone.

EUGENE. (*Sit Center table.*) That's not true. I know you—I know Laura.

BEN. Listen to him! No matter what arms may clasp us, what heart may warm us, what mouth may kiss us, we remain strangers. We never escape it. Never, never, never. (*Closes eyes, leans back.*)

EUGENE. Ben! Hey, Ben? (*Worriedly crosses Down to* BEN, *feels his face.*) Ben, you're burning up! Come on— (*Tries to lift him.*) Put your arms around me. I'm going to take you home.

BEN. (*Sinks back.*) Can't. It's all right, I'm just tired.

EUGENE. (*Takes* BEN's *coat from his lap and puts it around his shoulders.*) Why didn't you tell somebody you're sick, you crazy idiot! (*Again tries to lift* BEN.)

BEN. To hell with them, Gene. To hell with them all. Don't give a damn for anything. Nothing gives a damn for you. There are a lot of bad days, there are a lot of good ones— (EUGENE *rushes into the office, picks up the telephone.*) That's all there is . . . a lot of days . . . My God, is there no freedom on this earth?

EUGENE. (*Into telephone.*) Get me Dr. Maguire quickly. *It's my brother Ben!*

BEN. (*Stirs, in anguish, looks up at the Carrara angel.*) And still you smile. . . .

CURTAIN

ACT TWO

SCENE 2

SCENE: *The Dixieland Boarding House; the next night. A painful tenseness grips the house.* LAURA *and* EUGENE *sit together on the yard seat Down Left.* MRS. PERT *sits motionless in a rocker near the front door.* HUGH *slowly walks about. The inside hall is lighted; as is* BEN's *room, which we see for the first time. There* DR. MAGUIRE *and* HELEN *are hovering over* BEN'S *still body.* GANT *is at the hall telephone.*

GANT. (*Shouting into telephone.*) Second class seaman, Luke Gant. G-A-N-T—Gant! (*Angrily.*) I don't know why you can't hear me.

HUGH. (*Crosses to door.*) W.O., you don't have to shout because it's long distance.

GANT. Shut up, Hugh, I know what I'm doing. (*Into telephone.*) Do what? I am standing back from the telephone. All right, all right. . . . (*Moves telephone away from him, lower.*) Can you hear me now? Of all the perversities. Very well, I will repeat. Yesterday I sent a telegram to my son, Luke Gant, to come home, that his brother Ben has pneumonia. Can you tell me if—oh, he did leave? Why didn't he let us know? All right! Thank you. Thank you very much. (*Hangs up, joins the* OTHERS *on the veranda.*)

HUGH. They gave him leave?

GANT. If he made good connections he ought to be here by now.

HUGH. Ben'll be all right, W.O.

GANT. (*Crosses to sit wicker stool Down Right.* HUGH *sits woodbox.*) I remember when little Grover was ill in St. Louis, and Eliza sent for me. I didn't get there on time.

ELIZA. (*Enters from the house.*) Did you reach him?

GANT. He's on his way.

ELIZA. (*At Center on porch.*) It's all nonsense, of course. Ben is far from dying. But you do like to dramatize, Mr. Gant. Still, it will be good to see Luke—

EUGENE. (*Crosses to* ELIZA.) Mama, when can I see Ben?

ELIZA. When the doctor says. I'll tell you what: when you go in there, don't make out like Ben is sick. Just make a big joke of it—laugh as big as you please—

EUGENE. (*Groans, sits Left of Left pillar.*) Mama!

ELIZA. Well, it's the sick one's frame of mind that counts. I remember when I was teaching school in Hominy township, I had pneumonia. Nobody expected me to live, but I—did—I got through it somehow. I remember one day I was sitting down—I reckon I was convalescing, as the fella says. Old Doc Fletcher had been there—and as he left I saw him shake his head at my cousin Sally. "Why, Eliza, what on earth," she says, just as soon as he had gone, "he tells me you're spitting up blood every time you cough; you've got consumption as sure as you live!" "Pshaw!" I said. I remember I was just determined to make a big joke of it. "I don't believe a word of it," I said. "Not one single word." And it was because I didn't believe it that *I got well.*

GANT. (*Quietly.*) Eliza, don't run on so.

HELEN. (*Appears on veranda.*) The doctor says Mama can come in for a few minutes, but no one else yet.

EUGENE. (*Rises, take* HELEN's *hand.*) How is he?

HELEN. You know Dr. Maguire. If you can get anything out of him. . . . (ELIZA *takes a big breath; she and* HELEN *go in.*)

GANT. (*Moans worriedly.*) Oh God, I don't like the feel of it. I don't like the feel of it.

BEN. (*Weakly.*) Maguire, if you don't stop hanging over me I'll smother to death.

MAGUIRE. (*To the* WOMEN *as they enter.*) With both of you in here soaking up oxygen, leave that door open. (ELIZA *advances slowly to* BEN, *swallows a gasp at the sight of the tortured, wasted body.* BEN's *eyes are closed.*)

HELEN. (*Foot of bed.*) Mama's here, Ben.

ELIZA. (*Speaking as though to a baby.*) Why hello, son—did you think I wasn't ever coming in to see you?

HELEN. (*After a pause.*) Ben, Mama's here.

ELIZA. (*To* MAGUIRE.) Can't he talk? Why doesn't he look at me?

MAGUIRE. (*Head of bed.*) Ben, you can hear what's going on, can't you?

BEN. (*Quietly, his eyes still closed.*) I wish you'd all get out and leave me alone.

ELIZA. What kind of talk is that? You have to be looked after, son!

BEN. Then let Mrs. Pert look after me.

HELEN. Ben!

BEN. Maguire, where's Fatty? I want to see Fatty.

HELEN. (*Crosses Center of bed.* ELIZA *turns away Up Left.*) Ben, how can you talk that way? Your mother and your sister? If it weren't for that woman you wouldn't be sick now. Drinking, carousing with her night after night—

BEN. (*Yells with dwindling strength.*) Fatty! Fatty! (*On the veranda* MRS. PERT *stands quickly, then enters house toward* BEN'S *room.*)

HELEN. (*To* BEN.) You ought to be ashamed of yourself!

DR. MAGUIRE. Mrs. Gant, we need some more cold cloths. Why don't you—

HELEN. (*Crosses angrily to* MAGUIRE.) Fiend! Do you have to add to her misery? When you need something, ask me. (ELIZA *starting out of* BEN'S *room, meets* FATTY *in doorway.* FATTY *hesitates.*)

DR. MAGUIRE. That's all right, Mrs. Pert.

BEN. (*Immediately turns toward her.*) Fatty?

DR. MAGUIRE. Ben seems to want you here, that's all I care about. (*To* HELEN.) You'll be called if you're needed.

HELEN. This is the last time you come into this house, Dr. Maguire!

(HELEN *leaves the room. Outside* BEN'S *door* ELIZA *hands some cold cloths to* HELEN.)

BEN. Fatty, stay by me. Sing to me. "A Baby's Prayer at Twilight."

FATTY. (*Sitting beside him.*) Sh-h-h, Ben. Be quiet, dear. Save yourself.

BEN. Hold my hand, Fatty.

FATTY. (*Takes his hand, sings.*)*

* "Just a Baby's Prayer at Twilight," words by Sam M. Lewis

"Just a baby's prayer at twilight
When lights are low
A baby's years
Are filled with tears
Hmmmmm hmmmmm hmmmmmm."

(HELEN *re-enters* BEN'S *room. Places cloths on bureau. Hearing the voice,* EUGENE *stands, looks up toward* BEN'S *room.* HELEN *and* ELIZA *appear on the veranda,* HELEN *comforting her mother.*)

EUGENE. How does he seem, Mama?

ELIZA. (*Right of* HELEN.) He couldn't stand to see me worrying. That's what it was, you know. He couldn't stand to see me worrying about him.

GANT. (*Groaning.*) Oh Jesus, it's fearful—that this should be put on me, old and sick as I am—

HELEN. (*In blazing fury. Crosses to Left of him.*) You shut your mouth this minute, you damned old man! I've spent my life taking care of you! Everything's been done for you—everything—and you'll be here when we're all gone—so don't let us hear anything about your sickness, you selfish old man—it makes me furious!

DR. MAGUIRE. (*Appearing on veranda.*) If any of you are interested, Ben is a little better.

EUGENE. Thank God!

HELEN. Ben is better? Why didn't you say so before?

ELIZA. I could have told you! I could have told you! I had a feeling all along!

DR. MAGUIRE. (*Crosses down steps.*) I'll be back in a little while.

GANT. Well! We can all relax now.

DR. MAGUIRE. (*Motions* EUGENE *away from the others*

---

and Joe Young, music by M. K. Jerome. © 1918. Copyright renewal 1946. Mills Music, Inc., and Warlock Music, Inc. Used by permission of the copyright owners solely for the purpose of printing in this edition. CAUTION: Permission to include this song in any performance of this play must be obtained from Belwin Mills Publishing Corp., 16 W. 61st Street, New York, N. Y. 10023.

to Down Left.) Eugene, it's both lungs now. I can't tell them. But see to it that they stay around. I'm going next door and phone for some oxygen. It may ease it a little for him. It won't be long. (*He gives* EUGENE *a fond, strengthening touch, exits.*)

GANT. (*In doorway.*) What about Luke? Luke'll be furious when he finds out he came all this way for nothing!

ELIZA. (R. *of him.*) For nothing? You call Ben's getting well "for nothing"?

GANT. Oh, you know what I mean, Miss Eliza. I'm going to take a little nap.

ELIZA. You're going to take a little nip, that's what you mean.

GANT. You can come up and search my room if you don't believe me. (*Exits into house.*)

(EUGENE *stands, dazed and miserable, forces himself during the following scene.* JAKE *and* FLORRY *enter from rear veranda where* HELEN *and* HUGH *have moved to.*)

ELIZA. (*Excitedly.*) Mr. Clatt, Miss Mangle—did you hear? Ben is getting better! The crisis is past!

JAKE. We're so happy for you, Mrs. Gant.

ELIZA. I knew all along—something told me. Oh, not that he didn't have a very high fever—I admit that—but my second sense—

LUKE. (*Off Right.*) Hello—o—o there!

ELIZA. (*Peering off.*) Luke! (*Rushes down steps.*) Luke! Luke Gant!

(*The* BOARDERS *melt into the background as* LUKE GANT *enters, wearing a Navy uniform and carrying a lightly packed duffle bag, which he places on wicker stool Down Right. He is attractive, slight, lighted by an enormous love of humor and life, and adored by everyone. He is the son who got away early, but he still carries the marks of a distressing childhood; he sometimes stutters.*)

LUKE. Mama, Mama! (*Swings her around.*)

HUGH. (*Right of him in yard.*) Well, if it isn't the sailor himself! How are you?

LUKE. (*Shaking hands with* HUGH.) I'm fine, Hugh! How goes it?

ELIZA. Aren't you going to kiss your old mother?

LUKE. Old? You're getting younger and stronger by the minute. (*Kisses her.*)

ELIZA. I am, I am, son. I feel it—now that Ben's going to get well.

LUKE. The old boy is better?

HELEN. (R. *of* R. *pillar.*) Luke!

LUKE. Helen!

HELEN. (*Leaps into his arms from porch.*) How's my boy?

LUKE. S-s-slick as a puppy's belly. I thought you all might need cheering up. I brought you some ice cream from Woodruff's! (*Gives carton of ice cream to* HELEN.)

HELEN. Naturally; you wouldn't be Luke Gant if you didn't!

EUGENE. (*Crosses to Center.*) Welcome home, Luke!

LUKE. (*Crosses to him. They shake hands.*) My God, doesn't anybody buy you any clothes—and look at that hair. Mama, he looks like an orphan! Cut off those damn big feet of his, he'd go up in the air!

EUGENE. How long have you got, Luke?

LUKE. Can you s-s-stand me for twenty-four hours? (*Sees* LAURA, *crosses to her.*) Who's this?

ELIZA. (*Following.*) That's Miss James from Virginia. Laura, this is another of my sons, Luke Gant.

LAURA. (*Shaking hands.*) How do you do, Mr. Gant?

LUKE. How do you do?

ELIZA. (*Drawing* LUKE *away.*) All right, just come along here, and behave yourself.

HELEN. I'd better dish up the ice cream before it melts. (*Exits into house.*)

LUKE. (*Calling after* HELEN *from porch.*) Maybe Ben would like some. I got pistachio especially for him.

ELIZA. (*To* HELEN, *Left of Left pillar.*) Tell your father the admiral is here!

LUKE. Can I see Ben, now?

ELIZA. Well, the truth is, that Mrs. Pert is in there with him now.

LUKE. Mrs. Pert is? (*Looks at the* OTHERS.)

HUGH. (*Crosses onto porch with duffle bag. Sits wood-box.*) I wouldn't go into it, Luke. It's a somewhat "fraught" subject.

LUKE. Oh boy, oh boy, I know what that is! Still the same old happy household? (LUKE *and* ELIZA *sit on the veranda edge.*)

ELIZA. Nonsense. I have nothing against the woman except she's getting too many ideas that she's a fixture here. First thing in the morning I'm going to ask her to move.

LUKE. Doesn't she pay her rent?

ELIZA. Oh, she pays it.

LUKE. (*Laughs.*) Then you're never going to ask her to move—don't kid me! The paying customers are what counts around here! Aren't they, Mama?

ELIZA. Luke Gant, there are certain standards I have to keep up, for the reputation of Dixieland!

LUKE. (*Never unkindly.*) What kind of standards? The old dope fiend who hung himself in the same bedroom where Ben had to sleep for eight years after he cut him down? And all those amateur femme fatales who bask under your protection here, waylaying us in the hall, the bathroom—Mama, we never had a s-s-safe moment! And people think you find out about life in the Navy!

ELIZA. (*Playfully.*) I'm warning you, Luke! It's a good thing I know you're teasing.

(HELEN *enters with plates, dishes up ice cream.*)

LUKE. Remember the early mornings when Ben and Gene and I used to take the paper route together, remember, Gene? Old Ben used to make up stories for us about all the sleeping people in all the sleeping houses! He always used to throw the papers as lightly as he could because he hated to wake them. Remember, Gene?

HELEN. (*Offering* HUGH *ice cream.*) And that book of baseball stories Ben used to read to us by the hour—what was it, Gene?

EUGENE. (*In tears.*) *You know me, Al,* by Ring Lardner.

ELIZA. (*Leaping to* EUGENE.) Eugene. Child, what is it? What is it!

MRS. PERT. (*Enters hurriedly.*) Mrs. Gant! Mrs. Gant!

HELEN. What is it, Mrs. Pert?

MRS. PERT. He can't get his breath!

HUGH. Gene, get the doctor! (HELEN *and* ELIZA *follow* MRS. PERT *into the house.*)

ELIZA. You ridiculous woman! The doctor said he was better. (EUGENE *exits to get* DR. MAGUIRE. GANT *enters side door.*)

GANT. What the hell's all the commotion about? (*Sees* LUKE.) Luke! Welcome home!

LUKE. (*As they shake hands Right Center.*) Papa—Ben's not doing so well.

GANT. (*Crosses to Right pillar.*) Jesus, have mercy! That I should have to bear this in my old age. Not another one—first Grover, now Ben . . .

LUKE. (*On porch above him.*) For God's sake, Papa, try to behave decently, for Ben's sake! (EUGENE *and* DR. MAGUIRE *enter hurriedly.*)

GANT. (*Seizing* DR. MAGUIRE.) Maguire, you got to save him—you got to save him. (DR. MAGUIRE *pushes past* GANT *into the house, enters* BEN'S *room where the three women are gathered,* MRS. PERT *standing nearest* BEN *at the head of the bed.*)

DR. MAGUIRE. You women step back, give him air. (*Bends over* BEN.)

GANT. (*Collapsing on to the porch Right of Right pillar.*) When the old die, no one cares. But the young . . . the young . . .

EUGENE. (*Sits Left of him on steps.* LUKE *sits rocker.*) I would care, Papa.

BEN. It's one way—to step out of—the photograph—isn't it, Fatty?

FATTY. Hush, Ben, don't say that!

HELEN. (*To* DR. MAGUIRE; *Right of him.*) There must be something you can do!

DR. MAGUIRE. (*Straightens up.*) Not all the king's horses, not all the doctors in the world can help him now.

HELEN. Have you tried everything? Everything?

DR. MAGUIRE. (*Turns Upstage.*) My dear girl! He's drowning! Drowning!

ELIZA. (*In deep pain, moving from foot of bed.*) Mrs. Pert, you're standing in my place— (FATTY *moves away.* ELIZA *steps close to* BEN, *sits.*) Ben—son.

(*She reaches to touch him. His head turns toward her, drops. There is a last rattling, drowning sound.* BEN *dies.* DR. MAGUIRE *checks his heart.*)

DR. MAGUIRE. It's over. It's all over.

HELEN. (*Racked, exits to veranda; tries to stifle her sobs.*) He's gone. Ben's gone.

(ELIZA *sits stool and takes* BEN'S *hand.* FATTY *puts the socks she has been knitting at* BEN'S *feet and exits upstairs.* HELEN *falls into* EUGENE'S *arms.* DR. MAGUIRE, *carrying his doctor's bag, appears in the hall, puts a match to his chewed cigar.*)

EUGENE. (*Crossing to Right of* DR. MAGUIRE.) Did he say anything? Did he say anything at the end?

DR. MAGUIRE. What were you expecting him to say?

EUGENE. I don't know. I just wondered.

DR. MAGUIRE. If he found what he was looking for? I doubt that, Gene. At least he didn't say anything.

(EUGENE *leaves and goes into* BEN'S *room.* DR. MAGUIRE *comes out into the veranda.*)

LUKE. How long have you known, Doc?

DR. MAGUIRE. For two days—from the beginning. Since I first saw him at three in the morning in the Uneeda Lunch with a cup of coffee in one hand and a cigarette in the other.

GANT. Was there nothing to be done?

DR. MAGUIRE. My dear, dear Gant, we can't turn back the days that have gone. We can't turn back to the hours when our lungs were sound, our blood hot, our bodies young. We are a flash of fire—a brain, a heart, a spirit. And we are three cents' worth of lime and iron—which we cannot get back. (*He shakes his head.*) We can believe in the nothingness of life. We can believe in the nothingness of death, and of a life after death. But who can believe in the nothingness of Ben?

HELEN. Come on, Papa, there's nothing more to sit up for. Let me put you to bed. Come along.

(*She takes the* OLD MAN *and leads him gently into the house, as* DR. MAGUIRE *exits.* HUGH *and* LUKE *exit after* HELEN *and* GANT. *Only* LAURA *is left, still sitting on the yard seat,* EUGENE, *who has been standing in the corner in* BEN'S *room, goes to his* MOTHER, *who is holding* BEN'S *hand tightly.*)

EUGENE. Mama?

ELIZA. He doesn't turn away from me any more.

EUGENE. (*Takes her hand, tries gently to disengage* BEN'S.) Mama, you've got to let go. You've got to let go, Mama! (ELIZA *shakes her head, her rough clasp tightening.* EUGENE *leaves the room, comes out to the veranda. There, slowly, he sinks to his knees, prays.* LAURA *watches him, her heart going out to him.*) Whoever You are, be good to Ben tonight. Whoever You are, be good to Ben tonight . . . Whoever You are . . . be good to Ben tonight . . . be good to Ben tonight. . . .

SLOW CURTAIN

ACT THREE

SCENE: *The Dixieland Boarding House; two weeks later.
The house is seen in a SOFT EARLY LIGHT. From
Offstage, a NEWSBOY, whistling, throws four
tightly wadded newspapers onto the veranda—
plop—plop—plop—plop. The whistling and his steps
fade away. The LIGHTS come up dimly in LAURA's
room. LAURA is in bed in her nightgown. EUGENE is
at the foot of the bed by the window, looking out.
He takes his shirt from the bedpost, puts it on.*

LAURA. (*Stirring.*) Gene? What was that?

EUGENE. (*Head of* LAURA's *bed.*) Soaks Baker with
the morning papers. Plop-plop-plop-plop—how I used to
love that sound. Every time the heavy bag getting lighter.
I'll always feel sorry for people who have to carry things.
(*Sighs.*) It's getting light, it's nearly dawn.

LAURA. Don't go yet. (*Reaches for his hand.*)

EUGENE. Do you think I want to on your last morning
here? Mama gets up so early. Do you know that every
morning before she cooks breakfast she visits Ben's
grave? (*Sits on bed, takes her in his arms.*)

LAURA. Gene, Gene.

EUGENE. Oh Laura, I love you so. When I'm close to
you like this, it's so natural. Are all men like me? Tell me.

LAURA. I've told you I've never known anyone like you.

EUGENE. (*As* LAURA *turns away.*) But you have known
men? It would be strange if you hadn't. A woman so
beautiful, so loving. You make me feel like I only used
to dream of feeling. I've hardly thought to daydream in
weeks—except about us.

LAURA. What did you used to dream?

EUGENE. I always wanted to be the winner, the general,
the spearhead of victory! Then following that I wanted to
be loved. Victory and love! Unbeaten and beloved. And
I am that now, truly! Laura, will you marry me?

LAURA. (*Moving away.*) Oh, darling!

EUGENE. You knew I was going to ask you, didn't you? You knew I couldn't let you go even for a day.

LAURA. Yes, I knew.

EUGENE. You're happy with me. You know I make you happy. And I'm so complete with you. Do you know that three hundred dollars Ben left me? He would want me to use it for us. I'll go with you to Richmond today. I'll meet your parents, so they won't think I'm an irresponsible fool who's stolen you. That may be a little hard to prove —but there is a job I can get. Would you mind living in Altamount?

LAURA. (*Moving into his arms.*) I don't care where I live. Just keep holding me.

EUGENE. I am going to have to tell Mama first.

LAURA. Let's not worry about that now. Tell me about us.

EUGENE. All the treasures the world has in store for us? We'll see and know them all. . . . All the things and the places I've read about. There isn't a state in this country we won't know. The great names of Arizona, Texas, Colorado, California—we'll ride the freights to get there if we have to. And we'll go to Europe, and beyond—the cool, green land of Shakespeare, the gloomy forests of Gaul, the great Assyrian plains where Alexander feasted —the crumbling walls of Babylon, the palaces of the kings of Egypt, the towering white crags of Switzerland. My God, Laura, there might not be time enough for all!

LAURA. There will be time enough, darling.

(*From a far distance, they hear the WHISTLE of a train as it passes.*)

EUGENE. The Richmond train leaves at noon. I'll have to get packed.

LAURA. You do love trains, don't you?

EUGENE. I love only you. Will you have confidence in me, the unbeaten and beloved?

LAURA. Yes, darling, I will have confidence in you.

EUGENE. I'll never have to sneak out of this room again. (*Rises, moves to the door.* LAURA, *on her knees, reaches toward him.*)

LAURA. Eugene! (*He comes back to her.*) I will love you always. (*They kiss.* EUGENE *exits.* LAURA *leaps from the bed, hurries after him.*) Gene!

(ELIZA *has come out the side door, putting on sweater, takes flowers out of a bucket preparing to take them to* BEN'S *grave.* EUGENE *enters the hallway, lifts the phone receiver. He doesn't see* ELIZA. *LIGHTS dim down on* LAURA'S *room as she gets slippers and exits.*)

EUGENE. (*Into telephone.*) Good morning. Three-two, please— Hello, Uncle Will? This is Eugene— Yes, I know how early it is— You know that position you offered me? I've decided to take it.

ELIZA. (*Pleased, to herself.*) Well, can you imagine!

EUGENE. (*Into telephone.*) I've thought it over, and that's what I'd like to do, for a while anyway— That's right— That's fine— Well, you see, I'm getting married— (ELIZA *freezes in pain at Center.*) Yes, married—to Miss James. We're going to Richmond for a few days. We're leaving on the noon train— Thanks, Uncle Will. Thanks a lot. (*Hangs up and starts to go back upstairs.*)

ELIZA. Eugene!

EUGENE. (*Coming out to her slowly.*) Well, now—with your second sense, I thought you would have guessed it, Mama.

ELIZA. (*Sits Left of Left pillar.*) Why didn't I know, why didn't I see?

EUGENE. (*Kneels at pillar.*) I'm sorry, Mama, but we couldn't wait any longer.

ELIZA. Gene, child, don't make this mistake. She's so much older than you. Don't throw yourself away, boy!

EUGENE. Mama, there's no use arguing. Nothing you can say will change my mind.

ELIZA. (*Desperately.*) And my plans for you? What of my plans for you?

EUGENE. Mama, I don't want your plans, I've got my own life to live! (*Moves to Right on porch.* ELIZA *follows.*)

ELIZA. But you don't know! Gene, listen, you know that Stumptown property of mine? I sold it just yesterday so you could go to Chapel Hill— You know I've always wanted you to have an education. You can have it now, child, you can have it.

EUGENE. It's too late, Mama, it's too late!

ELIZA. Why law, child, it's never too late for anything! It's what Ben wanted, you know.

EUGENE. Laura and I are leaving, Mama. I'm going up to get packed. (*She turns away from his kiss and he exits into house.*)

ELIZA. Gene! (ELIZA *stands looking after him a moment, then quickly enters the hall, lifts the telephone receiver.*) Three-two, please. (*Waits.*)

HELEN. (*Enters from the kitchen, with a broom with which she sweeps the veranda.*) What are you calling Uncle Will so early for?

ELIZA. (*Into phone.*) Will? No, no, I know—I heard— Yes, I know it's early— Listen, Will, I want you to do something for me. You know my Stumptown property? I want you to sell it— Now, this morning— Will, don't argue with me— I don't care what it's worth. Call Cash Rankin, he's been after me for weeks to sell— Well, I know what I want to do— I'll explain it to you later— Just do what I say and let me know. (*She hangs up.*)

(LAURA *re-enters her bedroom.*)

HELEN. Well, it's never too early in the morning to turn a trade, is it? What are you selling?

ELIZA. Some property I own.

HELEN. Maybe you can put a little of that money into getting somebody else to help you at that altar of yours, the kitchen stove.

ELIZA. (*Puts sweater on hall chair.*) Helen, get breakfast started, will you? I'll be in later. And if Gene comes down, keep him in there, will you?

HELEN. Oh, all right. You let me know when I can let him out! (*Exits into house.*)

(ELIZA *appears at door of* LAURA'S *room.* LAURA *is dressed and is packing her suitcase on the bed.*)

LAURA. Oh, Mrs. Gant. I've been expecting you. Come in. (*As* ELIZA *enters.*)

ELIZA. I should think you would.

LAURA. Mrs. Gant, before you say anything—

ELIZA. I'll vow I can't believe a mature woman—at a time of trouble like this—would take advantage of a child, a mere child—

LAURA. Mrs. Gant, will you please listen?

ELIZA. (*Tossing her nightgown from head of bed into suitcase.*) I will listen to nothing. You just pack your things and get out of this house. I should have known what you were from the first minute I set eyes on you . . . "I'm looking for a room, Mrs. Gant . . . " Why, butter wouldn't melt in your mouth—

LAURA. (*Slowly, distinctly.*) Mrs. Gant, I am not marrying Eugene. I'm not. I wish with all my heart I could!

ELIZA. (*Turning to dresser.*) You can't lie out of it. Gene just told me.

LAURA. I am engaged to be married to a young man in Richmond.

ELIZA. What kind of a wicked game are you playing with my child?

LAURA. (*Sits bed.* ELIZA *sits chair Left.*) Mrs. Gant, this isn't easy. I should have told Gene long ago—but I didn't. A girl about to get married suddenly finds herself facing responsibilities. I never liked responsibilities. Gene knows how I am. I like music, I like to walk in the woods, I like—to dream. I know I'm older than Gene, but in many ways I'm younger. The thought of marriage frightened me. I told my fiancé I needed time to think it over. I fell in love with Eugene. I found the kind of romance I'd never known before, but I've also found that it isn't the answer. Gene is a wonderful boy, Mrs. Gant. He must go to college. He must have room to expand and grow, to find himself. He mustn't be tied down at this point in his life. He needs the whole world to wander in—and I know now that I need a home, I need children—I need a husband. (*Rises, closes bag.*) For people like me there are rules, very good rules for marriage and for happiness—and I've broken enough of them. I telephoned Philip last night. He's arriving at the depot on that early train. We're going on to Charleston together, and we'll be married there. He loves me, and I will love him too after a while. (*Takes note from desk.*) I left this note for Eugene. I couldn't just tell him. (*Gives it to* ELIZA. *Crosses for bag, puts it Down Left of head of bed. Gets hat and purse from bureau.*) Will you say good-bye to Mr. Gant for me, and tell him I hope he feels better? And my good-byes to Mr. Clatt and the others? And to Helen. Especially to Helen. She works so hard. (*Looks around.*) Good-bye, little room. I've been happy here. (*Picks up suitcase, faces* ELIZA.) Some day you're going to have to let him go, too. Good-bye, Mrs. Gant. (*She exits.*)

(*During the above* HUGH *has entered the veranda, is seated, reading the newspaper.* LAURA *enters from the house, looks back lingeringly, then, hearing the approaching TRAIN, hurries Off toward the station Down Left.* HELEN *enters, drinking coffee.*)

HELEN. Mama? Now, where on earth! Hugh, have you seen Mama?

HUGH. Umph.

HELEN. (*Crosses Upstage on porch.*) Do you know she was on the phone just now selling some property? Imagine—at this hour! And she leaves me to slave in the kitchen. . . . Do you know where she is?

HUGH. You know, they don't advertise the good jobs in here, not the really big ones.

GANT. (*Entering in his suspenders, sleepily rubbing his jaw.*) Isn't breakfast ready yet?

HELEN. Papa, how many times has Mama told you, you wait until the boarders have had theirs! And don't you dare appear in front of them in your suspenders, do you hear?

GANT. Merciful God! What a way to greet the day! (*He exits.*)

HELEN. (*Calling after* GANT.) Papa, do you know where Mama is?

(HELEN *exits after* GANT. EUGENE *enters downstairs, carrying his suitcase, stops at* LAURA'S *door, knocks.* ELIZA *has just laid* LAURA'S *letter on the bed.*)

EUGENE. Laura? Laura? (*Enters to* ELIZA.) Mama! Where's Laura? Where is she?

ELIZA. She's gone.

EUGENE. Gone? Where?

ELIZA. She just walked out on you, child. Just walked out on you. (*Shakes her finger at him.*) I could have told you, the minute I laid eyes on her—

EUGENE. (*Seizing* ELIZA'S *hand.*) You sent her away.

ELIZA. I never did. She just walked out on you, child. (EUGENE *breaks for the door.* ELIZA *picks up the letter, runs after him.*) Gene! Eugene! Wait!

EUGENE. (*Runs Down to the veranda.*) Laura— (*Looks up street.*) Laura— (*As* HUGH *points toward station, starts off that way.*) Laura—

ELIZA. (*Entering, waving the letter.*) Wait! Wait! She left you this. Gene! (EUGENE *turns, sees the letter.*) She left you this. Read it, child. (EUGENE *crosses to* ELIZA, *takes the letter, reads it as the TRAIN is heard leaving station.*) You see, it's no use. It's no use. (EUGENE *crosses slowly to the yard seat, sits.* ELIZA *watches him.* HELEN *enters through the front door.*)

HELEN. Mama, there you are! Where have you been?

We've got to start getting breakfast. (*As* ELIZA *waves her to silence.*) What's the matter?

ELIZA. That Miss James. She and Eugene—

HELEN. (*Laughs.*) Oh my God, Mama, have you just found out about that? What about it?

ELIZA. She's gone.

HELEN. What?

ELIZA. She just walked out on him.

HELEN. (*Crosses to* EUGENE.) Oh ho, so that's it, is it? Has your girl gone and left you, huh? Huh? (*Tickles his ribs; he turns, clasps her knees.*) Why, Gene, forget about it! You're only a kid yet. She's a grown woman.

ELIZA. (*Crossing above to Left of* EUGENE.) Helen's right. Why, child, I wouldn't let a girl get the best of me. She was just fooling you all the time, just leading you on, wasn't she, Helen?

HELEN. You'll forget her in a week, Gene.

ELIZA. Why, of course you will. Pshaw, this was just puppy love. Like the fellow says, there's plenty good fish in the sea, as ever came out of it.

HELEN. Cheer up, you're not the only man got fooled in his life!

HUGH. (*From behind his paper.*) By God, that's the truth! (HELEN *and* ELIZA *glare at him.*)

ELIZA. Helen, go inside, I'll be in in a minute.

HELEN. Oh, all right. Hugh, you come in and help me. (HELEN *exits, followed by* HUGH.)

ELIZA. (*Sits beside* EUGENE, *his back still turned to her.*) Gene. You know what I'd do if I were you? I'd just show her I was a good sport, that's what! I wouldn't let on to her that it affected me one bit. I'd write her just as big as you please and laugh about the whole thing.

EUGENE. Oh, God, Mama, please, leave me alone, leave me alone!

ELIZA. Why, I'd be ashamed to let any girl get my goat like that. When you get older, you'll just look back on this and laugh. You'll see. You'll be going to college next year, and you won't remember a thing about it. (EUGENE *turns, looks at her.*) I told you I'd sold that

Stumptown property, and I have. This year's term has started already but next year—

EUGENE. Mama, *now! Now!* I've wasted enough time!

ELIZA. What are you talking about? Why you're a child yet, there's plenty of time yet—

EUGENE. (*Rises, walks about her, beggingly.*) Mama, Mama, what is it? What more do you want from me? Do you want to strangle and drown me completely? Do you want more string? Do you want me to collect more bottles? Tell me what you want! Do you want more property? Do you want the town? Is that it?

ELIZA. Why, I don't know what you're talking about, boy. If I hadn't tried to accumulate a little something, none of you would have had a roof to call your own.

EUGENE. (*Right Center.*) A roof to call our own? Good God, I never had a bed to call my own! I never had a room to call my own! I never had a quilt to call my own that wasn't taken from me to warm the mob that rocks on that porch and grumbles.

ELIZA. (*Rises, looking for an escape.*) Now you may sneer at the boarders if you like—

EUGENE. No, I can't. There's not breath or strength enough in me to sneer at them all I like. Ever since I was this high, and you sent me to the store for the groceries, I used to think, "This food is not for us—it's for them!" Mama, making us wait until they've eaten, all these years—feeding us on *their* leftovers—do you know what it does to us?—when it's you we wanted for us, *you* we needed for us. Why? Why?

ELIZA. (*Trembling.*) They don't hurt me like the rest of you do—they wouldn't talk to me like you are, for one thing. (*Starts toward side door.*)

EUGENE. Because they don't care—they're strangers. They don't give a damn about you! They'll talk like this about you behind your back—I've heard them do that plenty!

ELIZA. (*Turns.*) What? What? What kind of things do they say about me?

EUGENE. What does it matter what they say—*they* say!

Doesn't it matter to you what I say? (*Takes her in his arms, holds her.*)

ELIZA. (*Beginning to weep.*) I don't understand.

EUGENE. (*Releases her, moves away.*) Oh, it's easy to cry now, Mama, but it won't do you any good! I've done as much work for my wages as you deserve. I've given you fair value for your money, I thank you for nothing. (*Crosses Up to the veranda.*)

ELIZA. (*Crosses to Left of Left pillar.*) What's that? What are you saying!

EUGENE. I said I thank you for nothing, but I take that back. Yes, I have a great deal to be thankful for. I give thanks for every hour of loneliness I've had here, for every dirty cell you ever gave me to sleep in, for the ten million hours of indifference, and for these two minutes of cheap advice.

ELIZA. You will be punished if there's a just God in Heaven.

EUGENE. Oh, there is! I'm sure there is! Because I have been punished. By God, I shall spend the rest of my life getting my heart back, healing and forgetting every scar you put upon me when I was a child. The first move I ever made after the cradle was to crawl for the door. And every move I ever made since has been an effort to escape. And now, at last I am free from all of you. And I shall get me some order out of this chaos. I shall find my way out of it yet, though it takes me twenty years more—alone. (*Starts for door.*)

ELIZA. Gene! Gene, you're not leaving?

EUGENE. Ah, you were not looking, were you? I've already gone.

(EUGENE *exits into the house.* ELIZA *sits on the veranda edge, stunned.* GANT, *wearing a vest over his suspenders, enters.*)

GANT. Now do you suppose I can get some breakfast? (ELIZA *doesn't answer.*) Well, do you mind if I make a fire in the fireplace? (*Goes to wood box, muttering.*) If I can't get any food to keep me alive, I can get a little warmth out of this drafty barn! (*Starts collecting wood from box.*) Some day I'm going to burn up this house— just pile in all the logs that old grate'll hold—and all the furniture—and all the wooden-headed people around here—and some kerosene—till this old barn takes off like a giant cinder blazing through the sky. That would show them—all fifteen miserable rooms—burning, blistering—

ELIZA. I wish you would, Mr. Gant. I just wish you would.

GANT. You think I'm joking.

ELIZA. No, I don't.

GANT. If I just get drunk enough, I will!

ELIZA. (*Rises, faces house.*) Serve it right—miserable, unholy house!

GANT. Why, Miss Eliza!

ELIZA. I'll do it myself— (*With demoniacal strength she shakes the Left pillar by the steps.*) I'll tear you down! I'll kill you, house, kill you! I'll shake you to pieces!

GANT. Let me help you, Mrs. Gant! (*Picks up* MRS. PERT'S *rocker, crashes it.*)

HELEN. (*Entering hurriedly.*) Eliza Gant, have you gone mad!

GANT. (*Drops wood, starts tearing at the other post.*) God-damned barn! Thief! Travesty on nature!

ELIZA. God-damned barn! (*Hits latticed panels under the veranda Left with stick of wood.*)

HELEN. (*Calls inside.*) Hugh, come out here!

WILL. (*Entering from rear of veranda.*) My God, what are they doing?

GANT. (*Screaming up at house. Brandishing torn pillar.*) Clatt—Mangle—Brown— Come out of there, you rats, all of you—come out, come out, wherever you are!

(THE BOARDERS *begin to yell and squeal from inside.*)

ELIZA. (*Hysterically imitating* GANT; *crossing Left.*) Come out, come out, wherever you are!

HUGH. (*Entering.*) What's going on?

GANT. (*Breaking off the newel post; crosses to Right Center.*) We're tearing down this murderous trap, that's what. Hand me the hatchet, Hugh. It's in the woodbox.

HUGH. Fine! Fine! (*Dashes to woodbox, takes out hatchet.*)

(BOARDERS *enter downstairs in various stages of undress.*)

BROWN. Call the police.

MRS. CLATT. Let's get to Mrs. Haskell's!

JAKE. Gant's off his nut!

GANT. (*Chasing them off Left, threatening the* BOARDERS.) Squeal, you croaking bastards. Croak and run! Run for your lives!

BOARDERS. (*Ad lib as they scurry off.*)

    The house is falling down!

    It's a tornado!

    Ladies' Temperance Society, humph!

    Has anyone called the police?

    (*Etc.*)

HUGH. (*Yard Right Center.*) Here's the hatchet, W.O.

GANT. (*Leaping for it. Tossing pillar Up Right Center.*) Give it to me.

WILL. (*Right of* HUGH, *grabbing for hatchet.*) Stop it, Gant—stop this! Have you all lost your minds?

ELIZA. (*Throwing flower pot after the* BOARDERS.) Go to Mrs. Haskell's!

HELEN. Mama!

GANT. (*Brandishing hatchet at* JAKE *and* MRS. CLATT *as they exit porch Up Right.*) Look at 'em run! And they haven't even had breakfast. Run, scatterbrains, empty-bellies!

JAKE. I'll sue you for this, Gant, I'll sue you for this! (*Exits.*)

(MRS. SNOWDEN *enters through front door.* GANT *whirls on her.*)

GANT. So you don't like the food here? So you don't like my wife's coffee! (MRS. SNOWDEN, *screaming, hastily retreats.*)

ELIZA. (*Lifting a chair to hurl after the* BOARDERS.) Why, law, that's good coffee! (HELEN *seizes* ELIZA'S *arms, stops her.* ELIZA'S *sensibilities slowly return.*)

GANT. Look at 'em run! Oh, Miss Eliza, what a woman you are! (*Roaring with laughter, he crosses down to* ELIZA, *is about to embrace her, sees her sober, shocked face.*)

ELIZA. (*Picking up broken pillar.*) Mr. Gant, Mr. Gant, what have you done? What have you done?

GANT. What have I done? What have I— Merciful God, woman!

ELIZA. (*Tosses pillar onto porch Left.*) Just look at this mess! And the boarders have all gone!

HELEN. (*Left of* ELIZA.) I don't know what got into you, Papa.

GANT. (*Speechless, turns to* HUGH *on porch Right.*) Merciful God! What got into me? Didn't she just stand there herself and—

ELIZA. Helen, go get the boarders, tell them he's been drinking, tell them anything, but get them back!

WILL. (*Down Right.*) I never saw such an exhibition.

ELIZA. Will, go with Helen. Tell them we all apologize. They'll listen to you. Hugh, help me clean up this mess. (HELEN *and* WILL *exit after the* BOARDERS *Up Right.*)

GANT. Let them go, Miss Eliza. *Let the boarders go!* (ELIZA *stands rigid.* GANT *waits anxiously.*)

ELIZA. (*On porch Center.*) I just don't know what came over me.

GANT. (*Crosses—flings the hatchet in the wood-box.* ELIZA *crosses to see damage to veranda lattice.*) Merciful God! (EUGENE *enters with his suitcase.*) Where are you going?

EUGENE. I'm going to school at Chapel Hill, Papa.

GANT. You are? (*He looks at* ELIZA.)

EUGENE. Mama promised me the money. She sold her Stumptown property.

GANT. (*Crosses to Right of her.*) Oh? By God, maybe it isn't going to be such a god-damned miserable day, after all! Got any money, son?

EUGENE. (*In yard, Right of* GANT.) I've got Ben's money. Thanks, Papa.

GANT. (*Takes money from his pocket, tucks it into* EUGENE'S *pocket.*) Well, go, Gene. Go for both of us. Keep right on going.

EUGENE. I will, Papa. Good-bye.

GANT. (*As they shake hands.*) Good-bye, Gene. (*Starts into house, turns.*) You're going to bust loose, boy— you're going to bust loose, all over this dreary planet!

(GANT *exits.* EUGENE *crosses to Right of* ELIZA, *who starts picking up the debris.*)

ELIZA. I reckon you've made up your mind all right.

EUGENE. Yes, Mama, I have. (*Crosses Down Left.*)

ELIZA. (*Crosses to porch, slamming wood in woodbox.*) Well, I'll deposit the money in the Chapel Hill Bank for you. I tell you what! It looks mighty funny, though, that you can't just stay a day or two more with Ben gone and all. It seems you'll do anything to get away from me. That's all right, I know your mind's made up and I'm not complaining! It seems all I've ever been fit for around here is to cook and sew. That's all the use any of you have ever had for me—

EUGENE. Mama, don't think you can work on my feelings here at the last minute.

ELIZA. It seems I've hardly laid eyes on you all summer long— (*Replacing wood in woodbox and picking up rocker.* EUGENE *turns to her.*) Well, when you get up there, you want to look up your Uncle Emerson and Aunt Lucy. Your Aunt Lucy took a great liking to you when they were down here, and when you're in a strange town it's mighty good sometimes to have someone you know. And say, when you see your Uncle Emerson, you might just tell him not to be surprised to see me any time now. (*She nods pertly at him.*) I reckon I can pick right up and light out the same as the next fellow when I get ready. I'm not going to spend all my days slaving away for a lot of boarders—it don't pay. If I can turn a couple of trades here this fall, I just may start out to see the world like I always intended to. I was talking to Cash Rankin the other day—he said, "Why, Mrs. Gant," he said, "if I had your head for figures, I'd be a rich man in—" (*Her talk drifts off.* EUGENE *stands looking at her. There is another terrible silence between them. She points at him with her finger, finally her old loose masculine gesture. Crossing to Left on porch.*) Here's the thing I'm going to do. You know that lot of mine on Sunset Terrace, right above Dick Webster's place? Well, I been thinking. If we started to build there right away, we could be in our own house by spring. I've been thinking about it a lot lately. . . . (*There is another silence.*) I hate to see you go, son.

EUGENE. Good-bye, Mama.

ELIZA. Try to be happy, child, try to be a little more happy. . . . (*She turns and, with unsteady step, starts into the house.*)

EUGENE. MAMA! (*He drops the valise, takes the steps in a single bound, catching* ELIZA's *rough hands, which she has held clasped across her body, and drawing them to his breast.*) GOOD-BYE . . . GOOD-BYE . . . GOOD-BYE . . . MAMA . . .

ELIZA. (*Holding him.*) Poor child . . . poor child . . . poor child. (*Huskily, faintly.*) We must try to love one another. (*Finally* EUGENE *moves from her, picks up the valise, as the LIGHTS start dimming, holding a SPOT on her.* ELIZA *seems to recede in the distance as into his memory.*) Now for Heaven's sake, spruce up, boy, spruce up! Throw your shoulders back! And smile, look pleasant! Let them know up there that you *are* somebody!

(ELIZA's *voice fades, the set is black. A SPOT holds on* EUGENE.)

EPILOGUE

BEN'S VOICE. So you're finally going, Gene?

EUGENE. Ben? Is that you, Ben?

BEN'S VOICE. Who did you think it was, you little idiot? Do you know why you're going, or are you just taking a ride on a train?

EUGENE. (*Looking up and front Right.*) I know. Of course I know why I'm going. There's nothing here for me. Ben, what really happens? Everything is going. Everything changes and passes away. Can you remember some of the things I do? I've already forgotten the old faces. I forget the names of people I knew for years. I get their faces mixed. I get their heads stuck on other people's bodies. I think one man has said what another said. And I forget. There is something I have lost and can't remember.

BEN'S VOICE. The things you have forgotten and are trying to remember is the child that you were. He's gone, Gene, as I am gone. And will never return. No matter where you search for him, in a million streets, in a thousand cities.

EUGENE. Then I'll search for an end to hunger, and the happy land!

BEN'S VOICE. Ah, there is no happy land. There is no end to hunger!

EUGENE. Ben, help me! You must have an answer. Help me, and I won't go searching for it.

BEN'S VOICE. You little fool, what do you want to find out there?

EUGENE. *I want to find the world. Where is the world?*

BEN'S VOICE. (*Fading.*) The world is nowhere, Gene.

. . .

EUGENE. Ben, wait! Answer me!

BEN'S VOICE. The world is nowhere, no one, Gene. *You* are your world.

(*The TRAIN WHISTLE sounds. LIGHTS reveal Dixie-land in dim silhouette.* EUGENE, *without looking back, exits.*)

CURTAIN

LOOK HOMEWARD, ANGEL

PROPERTY LIST

PRESET RIGHT PROP TABLE

Cigarettes and matches—BEN
Money—BEN
Real estate clippings and brochures
Geranium cuttings
2 potted plants
Handbag—ELIZA
Ukulele
Bill of sale   ⎰ One standby set
Check for $20,000.00   ⎱ One set for WILL
Pen—WILL (Standby in GANT's desk)
Picnic basket
Duffle bag with 1 quart of ice cream in it
4 folded newspapers
1 small bunch of autumn leaves
1 can of peat moss
Tray for small flower pots

PRESET LEFT PROP TABLE

Cane—MRS. CLATT
Umbrella—MISS BROWN
2 suitcases—LAURA, MR. FARREL—(Farrel's with
   strapped umbrella)
Handbag with vial of whiskey
Hankie
20 one dollar bills
1 Dixieland card
1 Doctor's bag with hypodermic, stethoscope, etc.
Cigars and matches—MAGUIRE
GENE's suitcase

ACT I—Scene 1

PRESET PORCH

4 chairs
1 rocking chair with: Knitting bag containing:
  Unfinished socks and poem
  Newspaper beside rocking chair
3 tables
1 woodbox with kindling and hatchet inside
Flower pots on railing
2 ashtrays and matches

PRESET HALL

1 table with telephone on it and Dixieland cards
  (in drawer)
1 small chair

PRESET GENE'S ROOM

(Check wall panels)
1 screen
1 table with books
1 chair with special book
1 footstool

PRESET GANT'S ROOM

(Check wall panels)
1 completely made bed with coverlet
  (GANT's robe and nightgown)

PRESET KITCHEN

1 tray with coffee service for 7
  7 cups, 7 saucers, 7 spoons
  7 napkins
  Sugar and creamer with spoon
  newspaper
1 coffee pot with 7 half-cups hot coffee
2 pot holders
2 dish cloths
1 broom—worn
2 cold cloths (small towels)

1 pitcher with water, 1 glass
1 cup with coffee
1 tray with ice cream service for 8
   8 dishes, 8 spoons, 8 napkins
   1 serving spoon
1 envelope (with map) and pencil

WARDROBE IN KITCHEN
   2 aprons

PRESET BACK YARD
   1 table with ashtray and matches
   2 chairs

STRIKE BETWEEN SCENES 1 & 2 IN FIRST ACT
   Newspaper from yard planter
   Tray and coffee cups from porch
   2 flower pots from yard table

ACT I—SCENE 2
Shoe and jacket (floor in Gant's room)
2 empty beer bottles)
2 glasses ½ full beer   porch Left
bottle opener)
Phono and records—Porch Right
1 capped bottle of beer—(garden seat)
Ben's jacket (hall chair)

ACT II—SCENE 1
DOWN LEFT UNIT
   1 stool
   1 desk with: 1 ledger, 1 book poems, 1 telephone
   1 apron on book Down Left (GANT)
   1 couchant lamb—Right of steps
   1 bench Right of unit
DOWN RIGHT UNIT
   On work bench:
      Stencils
      Pencils

Whetstone
Ruler
Tools
Worktable with slab Right Center, cloths on Right
     edge
1 chair behind worktable
1 small stool Down Right edge of unit
Egyptian urn under work bench
Gene's apron

WARDROBE OFF DOWN LEFT
Frock coat—high hat

PRESET MAIN HOUSE BETWEEN ACTS I & II
Ben's room—chair, bed, bureau and washstand
Basin with water on bureau
Cold cloths
Doctor's bag with stethoscope on washstand
Knitting on rocker (FATTY)

SET BETWEEN SCENES 1 and 2 ACT II
Yard:
    Stool Down Right
    Planter Left Center
    Chair Left of planter
    Down Left gardenseat unit

STRIKE BETWEEN ACT II & III
Center planter table

SET BETWEEN ACT II & III
Laura's room:
    Bed, chair, bureau
    Packed bag open on chair
    Note paper on bureau

COSTUME PLOT

ELIZA GANT: *Act 1, Scene 1*—Two piece dark green suit with yellow blouse. Black sailor straw hat. Black handbag. High laced black shoes. Take off jacket and hat before entering to greet Laura. *Scene 2*—Black and white checked house dress. Off-white apron with pocket. Hankie. *Act 2, Scene 1*—Shabby dark brown suit with matching soft wide-brimmed hat. Dark brown stole. *Scene 2*—Mauve print house dress. Black and white checked apron. Hankie. *Act 3*—Green and black house dress. Old brown sweater.

W. O. GANT: *Act 1, Scene 1*—Collarless off-white shirt with fine stripe. Grey trousers with subdued green and purple stripes. Suspenders. Work shoes. Vest worn open with watch and chain. *Scene 2*—Take off shoes, trousers, vest. Wear shirt in bed. *Act 2, Scene 1*—Trousers of tiny black and grey checks. Collarless white shirt. Vest. Later dons high wing collar and maroon tie. Bowler hat. *Act 2, Scene 2*—Same as first entrance in Act 2, Scene 1. *Act 3*—Same as second act. Remove vest for first entrance. Wear it for second entrance.

EUGENE GANT: *Act 1, Scene 1*—Worn grey-blue cord trousers. Collarless tan shirt. Tight black shoes. *Scene 2*—Same. Add soft collar, dirty sneakers. *Act 2, Scene 1*—Same. Add blue work apron. *Scene 2*—Same. *Act 3*—Same. Add frayed, outgrown, light-brown jacket for final entrance.

HELEN GANT: *Act 1, Scene 1*—Blue print house dress. Off-white apron. *Act 2, Scene 2*—Blue-green house dress. *Act 3*—First act costume.

BEN GANT: *Act 1, Scene 1*—Brown tweed suit. Tan shirt. Tie. Black shoes. Sleeve garters. Suspenders. *Act 1, Scene 2*—Same. *Act 2, Scene 1*—Grey worsted suit. Pale blue shirt. Tie. Suspenders. Handkerchief. *Act 2, Scene 2*—Light grey pajama tops.

FATTY: *Act 1, Scene 1*—Pink dress. Earrings. Black shoes. *Act 1, Scene 2*—Same. *Act 2, Scene 2*—Plum dress with pink chiffon vest insert.

LAURA JAMES: *Act 1, Scene 1*—Gold traveling suit. Wide brimmed natural straw hat. Brown shoes. Gloves. Handbag. White blouse. *Act 1, Scene 2*—Full skirted, white, eyelet-cotton dress. *Act 2, Scene 1*—Flowered orchid and blue summer dress. Pink shoes. *Act 2, Scene 2*—Green skirt. Green blouse. *Act 3*—White nightgown. Bedroom slippers. Change to Act 1 travel suit.

WILL PENTLAND: Brown suit with vest. High shoes. Straw homberg. No change.

DR. MAGUIRE: Baggy brown tweed trousers. Mismated jacket, belted behind. Brown cap. High collared shirt. Watch and chain. No change.

MADAME ELIZABETH: Rich wine dress. Gloves. Wide brimmed soft straw hat with flowers. Parasol. Stylish shoes.

LUKE GANT: Blue U.S. Navy enlisted man's uniform.

HUGH BARTON: Grey-green suit. Suspenders. Very high collar on blue shirt. Black shoes. Bowtie. Remove jacket for last entrance in Act 3.

JAKE CLATT: *Act 1, Scenes 1 and 2. Act 2, Scene 2*—Sharp light blue suit with vest. Extremely high collar on blue shirt. Black shoes. *Act 3*—Red and black bath robe.

MRS. CLATT: *Act 1, Scenes 1 and 2*—Brick colored gown with lace sleeves. *Act 3*—Flowered wrapper over petticoat.

MRS. SNOWDEN: *Act 1, Scenes 1 and 2*—Cream lace frock. *Act 3*—Cream lace wrapper.

FLORRY MANGLE: *Act 1, Scenes 1 and 2. Act 2, Scene 2*—Cream middie blouse and pleated skirt with navy trim. Light shoes. Hankie. Hair bow. *Act 3*—Flowered wrapper.

TARKINTON: Frayed grey trousers. Odd vest. Collarless tan shirt. Derby.

MISS BROWN: *Act 1, Scenes 1 and 2*—Green frock with square cut neck. Green shoes. Parasol. *Act 3*—Frilly wrapper.

MR. FARREL: Light cream "ice cream" suit. Black shoes. High collar on white shirt. Sailor straw hat. Tie.

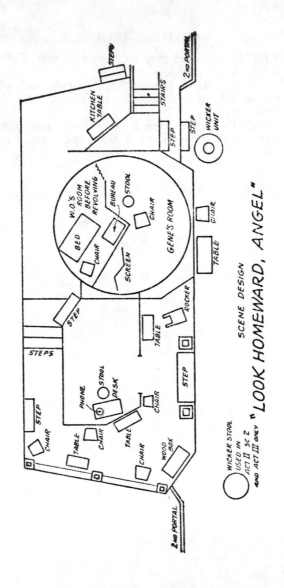

SCENE DESIGN

"LOOK HOMEWARD, ANGEL"

WICKER STOOL
USED IN
ACT II Sc 2
AND ACT III ONLY

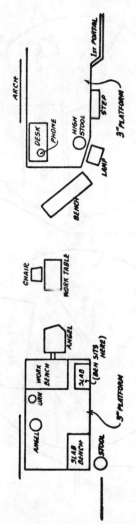

ACT II, -- SCENE I

SCENE DESIGN

"LOOK HOMEWARD, ANGEL"

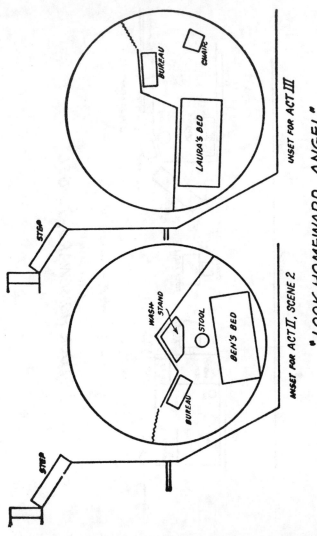

ONSET FOR ACT II, SCENE 2

WASH + STAND

STOOL

BEN'S BED

BUREAU

STEP

ONSET FOR ACT III

LAURA'S BED

BUREAU

CHAIR

STEP

"LOOK HOMEWARD, ANGEL"